ANDI DENCKLAU

10-Minute Dog Training Essentials

Science backed methods to build a strong bond, obedience and respect without needing to hire a dog trainer

Contents

1

Why Science-Backed Methods?

"Training isn't just about teaching commands; it's about building a relationship that transcends spoken language, turning brief moments into lasting bonds."
— Dr. John Paul Scott, Renowned Canine Behavior Researcher

* * *

73% of dog owners use some kind of training method.

* * *

Introduction to Canine Learning

Classical Conditioning

Classical conditioning involves the pairing of a neutral stimulus with an unconditioned stimulus to create a learned response. No bones about it!

For example, if a dog initially has no particular reaction to the sound of a bell (the neutral stimulus), but you repeatedly ring the bell just before offering the dog a treat (or as we canines like to think of it, "manna from heaven") the dog will start to associate the bell's sound with food. Over time, the dog will salivate (a conditioned response) when it hears the bell, even without food present. This is known as the conditioned response. Sounds like a drool-worthy situation, doesn't it?

It's a powerful tool in dog training and behavior modification, as it can be used to create positive or negative associations with various stimuli to shape a dog's behavior and responses. It's the Pavlovian equivalent of teaching an old dog new tricks!

The Paw-lov Experiments

Classical conditioning was first extensively studied by Russian physiologist Ivan Pavlov, not specifically in the context of dogs but with dogs as a key part of his experiments. Pavlov could have been considered the first dog whisperer, in a lab coat! In the late 19th and early 20th centuries, Pavlov conducted experiments with dogs to explore the principles of classical conditioning. He observed that dogs could be trained to associate a neutral stimulus (like a bell) with the delivery of food, leading to conditioned responses (like salivation) even when the food was not present. So, we owe our thanks to him for pioneering the "ring bell, get treat" training method.

Key Stages in Classical Conditioning

Classical conditioning involves several stages, which include:

- Unconditioned Stimulus (US): This is a stimulus that naturally triggers a specific response without any prior learning. For our canine pals, think of it as the "treat radar" kicking in.
- Unconditioned Response (UR): The unconditioned response is the innate or reflexive response that occurs in reaction to the unconditioned stimulus. Basically, it's the dog's way of saying, "Yum!"
- Conditioned Stimulus (CS): The conditioned stimulus starts as a neutral stimulus that, through association with the unconditioned stimulus, earns its "graduate degree" in getting a reaction.
- Conditioned Response (CR): This is the learned response that occurs when the conditioned stimulus is presented. In simple terms, it's when Fido hears the bell and thinks, "Did someone say treats?"

Applications in Dog Training

Creating positive emotional responses in your dog through classical conditioning involves pairing a treat with what initially may be a "ruff" situation.

First, identify what makes your dog's tail go between its legs—be it a vet visit, meeting new people, or the ominous rumble of thunder.

Next, choose something that makes your dog's tail wag, like treats, toys, or belly rubs. Apply this positive stimulus like a furry magician pulling treats out of a hat during these stressful situations.

The goal is to get your dog to associate the once-dreaded vacuum cleaner or vet clinic with a game of fetch or a tasty morsel.

Desensitization

Desensitization is like exposure therapy but for dogs. It's like teaching your dog that the vacuum cleaner isn't a monster that eats carpets and should be barked at incessantly.

Potential Pitfalls

In dog training, timing is so important it could practically be a fourth obedience command! A mistimed treat could be as confusing to a dog as a squirrel that suddenly stops running. Let me clarify upfront: When I talk about "negative" consequences, rest assured, I'm not suggesting you put your dog in the doghouse—literally or figuratively.

Pitfalls might include a stern "No!" or withholding that prized squeaky toy for a few moments, but physical punishment is an absolute no-go. Any form of physical harm is, in dog terms, a "bad human!"

In conclusion, classical conditioning is not just a scientific principle; it's a practical approach that even a dog could love—or at least salivate over. Done right, it makes for a well-behaved dog and a very happy human.

Operant Conditioning

Operant conditioning focuses on how a dog's behavior is shaped through consequences, including rewards and, yes, even the dreaded "no-no's." In this realm, dogs become little philosophers, learning to associate their actions with outcomes, which in turn, wag the tails of their future behavior.

Enter B.F. Skinner, the alpha of this psychological pack. He was a prominent American psychologist and behaviorist who would have probably been a dog's best friend, had he not been so busy making groundbreaking contributions to the field of psychology. Skinner's work, notably outlined in his must-reads for any canine enthusiast—"The Behavior of Organisms" (1938) and "Science and Human Behavior" (1953)—has had pawsitively profound impacts on how we understand learning in organisms, including Fido and friends. His theories are the foundation stones—or should we say, the chew toys—of modern behaviorism and have found applications far beyond psychology, making waves in animal training and education.

Let's fetch the four main components in operant conditioning:

1. Positive Reinforcement: Treats, anyone? This involves rewarding a dog with their version of a jackpot—like treats, praise, or play—right after they've performed a good-boy (or girl) action. For instance, treat in mouth when Rover sits on cue.
2. Negative Reinforcement: Ever heard of leash linguistics? This method involves removing an aversive tug to encourage good leash manners. A simple example: releasing leash tension when a dog stops pulling as if they're in the Iditarod.
3. Positive Punishment: This is where you add an unpleasant consequence to make a behavior as unpopular as the vet's office. For example, a stern "no" for treating the sofa like a chew toy.
4. Negative Punishment: Picture this, your dog jumps up, and you become as interactive as a statue. This method removes something enjoyable (like your attention) to discourage naughty canine antics.

Applications in Dog Training
Clicker training is more than just a fun way to annoy your neighbors.

It's a conditioned response system where a simple click becomes the canine equivalent of a high-five. Pair the clicker with a smorgasbord of rewards, and voila, Fido knows he's aced the test. You click when your dog offers the Oscar-worthy performance of 'sit' or 'stay,' followed by a treat faster than you can say "good dog!"

Here is a link to my favorite clicker that doesn't sound like you're calling aliens.

The starter kit for clicker training is simple: click, treat, repeat. Keep the loop going until you're convinced your dog thinks the clicker is a treat-dispensing deity. Then put it away, simmer down, and repeat later.

The next act involves suspense; click and let five seconds pass before the treat appears. This teaches your dog that patience is more than a virtue; it's a road to tasty rewards. Gradually stretch the treat-time gap, cementing in your dog's mind that a click is a treat IOU, redeemable upon good behavior.

A pro-tip for aspiring canine scholars: avoid treat training in a place that screams "snack time!" to your dog. For example, if your dog associates the kitchen with flying treats, train in a neutral zone. Pocket those treats in a sealed bag to sneak past those super-sniffers, and you're good to go!

Negative punishment, usually as popular as bath time, has its merits. For instance, if your social butterfly of a dog leaps onto you for attention, go into 'ignore mode,' thereby teaching them that jumping means a social snub.

Operant conditioning is not just textbook stuff; it's everyday dog parenting. Whether you're teaching "sit," "come," or "quit hogging the bed," positive reinforcement techniques play a leading role. Rewards flow like a well-placed game of fetch.

Leash training is like a dance; it's a combo of negative and positive reinforcement, where tension eases when your dog moonwalks by your side and treats fall when paws hit their mark.

Potential Pitfalls

Ah, the potholes on the training path. First, inconsistency is the enemy. If you're as unpredictable as a squirrel, your dog will be as confused as a cat at a dog show. This leads to behavioral chaos, not unlike a dog chasing its tail. So, keep the reward system as consistent as your dog's interest in the mailman.

Secondly, timing is of the essence. Imagine rewarding your dog five minutes after they sit; it's like laughing at a joke a week after you've heard it. Immediate rewards create that "Aha!" moment, reinforcing the right moves.

And finally, the dark side— excessive punishment can turn your loving pup into a stressed-out, jittery mess. If the dog starts viewing training sessions as a ticket to Stressville, not only does it slow learning, but it could also dampen the human-canine bond. And let's face it, that's a price too high for any dog lover to pay.

Cognitive learning in our furry friends is a fascinating journey into the depths of doggy intellect. Picture it: your four-legged companion, sitting there, pondering the mysteries of the universe (or at least the mysteries of the treat jar). But what exactly is cognitive learning in dogs?

Well, it's like this: cognitive learning is all about their ability to put on their thinking caps, so to speak. They're not just learning by instinct; they're flexing those mental muscles. It's like when you've got to solve a Rubik's Cube or figure out which remote controls the TV. Dogs do similar mental gymnastics.

Imagine your dog as a little Sherlock Holmes, solving canine mysteries left and right. They're like furry detectives, connecting the dots and figuring out the puzzle of life. How do they do it? It's all thanks to their nifty mental processes like reasoning, problem-solving, and memory.

Now, let's talk about memory for a moment. Dogs have pretty impressive recall abilities. They remember that squirrel they chased up a tree three months ago and dream about the day they might catch it. It's like having a library of experiences stored in their heads.

But cognitive learning goes beyond memory. Dogs are like mini scientists, conducting experiments in their heads. They observe, they learn, and they apply that knowledge. It's like when they figure out that if they nudge the treat jar with their nose, it might magically spill out tasty rewards. It's not just trial and error; it's strategic thinking.

Now, imagine a pack of wild dogs in a rugged wilderness. They're like an adventurous group of friends planning a cross-country road trip. But instead of highways, they've got rivers to navigate. There's this one river with a current that could rival a water park slide.

Enter the rookie, a young dog who's never seen this river before. He's like the newbie in the group, eager but clueless. So, he takes a plunge, thinking it's a piece of cake. But whoosh! The current grabs him like a theme park ride gone wrong. It's like he accidentally joined a whitewater rafting expedition.

Now, here comes the learning part. Our young adventurer doesn't just give up. No, sir! He remembers that wild ride and thinks, "Maybe there's a gentler route down this river." It's like learning from a roller coaster mishap and deciding to stick to the kiddie rides.

This whole cognitive learning thing isn't just for fun. It's the secret sauce in the world of dog training. Think of it as their superhero power. It allows them to grasp complex commands, tackle tricky problems, and handle challenging situations.

Imagine your dog as the James Bond of the canine world, always one step ahead, deciphering your every command with the precision of a secret agent defusing a bomb. Okay, maybe not that intense, but you get the idea.

Now, let's talk about dog puzzles. They're like the Sudoku of the doggy world. These clever contraptions make your dog put on their thinking cap. It's like giving them a little brain workout while they hunt for hidden treasures, AKA treats.

But hold your horses (or should I say, hold your paws). There's a catch when it comes to cognitive training. Too much of a good thing can lead to doggy frustration. Imagine trying to solve a Rubik's Cube with missing stickers; it's enough to make anyone throw in the towel.

So, when you're challenging your furry Einstein, start small and work your way up. It's like leveling up in a video game – you don't go from newbie to pro overnight.

And speaking of frustration, dogs can get as miffed as you do when you can't find your keys. Keep an eye out for signs like whining or giving up during training. That's your cue to hit the pause button and take it easy.

Lastly, let's talk about anthropomorphism. It's a big word that means treating your dog like a tiny human. We've all been guilty of it, like when we swear our dog understands every word of our rants about the weather. But let's face it; they're not mind readers. They've got their own unique way of thinking and solving problems, often driven by instincts and past experiences.

So, there you have it, cognitive learning in dogs. It's like a thrilling detective story, a mental obstacle course, and a treasure hunt all rolled into one. It's the secret to unlocking your dog's inner genius while sharing a few laughs along the way.

Why Science?

Picture this: Science-backed dog training methods are like the treasure map to unlock your dog's full potential. They're the well-researched, tried-and-true techniques that can turn your four-legged friend into the canine equivalent of a virtuoso. So, what makes these methods the cream of the training crop? Let's dig a little deeper.

Imagine you're embarking on a road trip with your dog, and you want to reach your destination smoothly. Science-backed training methods are like the trusty GPS that guides you along the way. They provide a clear route to your training goals, ensuring you and your furry co-pilot stay on the right path.

But it's not just about reaching your destination; it's about getting there consistently, every time. Think of these methods as the recipe for baking the perfect batch of cookies. When you follow the steps precisely, you get a delicious result every time. Similarly, science-backed training gives you a consistent, well-behaved dog.

Now, let's talk about communication. Ever tried having a conversation with someone who speaks a different language? It can be a frustrating experience. Traditional training methods can sometimes feel like you and your dog are speaking different languages. But with science-backed techniques, it's like you've cracked the code to doggy language. You understand each other perfectly, and that leads to a more harmonious relationship.

So, what's the secret sauce behind these methods? It's all about positive reinforcement. Picture yourself receiving a high-five every time you do something right. It's motivating, right? Well, that's exactly how positive reinforcement works for dogs. It creates a win-win situation, making training enjoyable for both you and your furry companion.

Now, let's dive into the ultimate showdown: science-backed methods vs. traditional training. Imagine two groups of dogs, each undergoing different training methods. It's like a battle of the training techniques, and we're about to see who comes out as top dog.

In one corner, we have the science-backed champions. They use positive reinforcement, understand dog behavior inside out, and prioritize building a strong bond. It's like they've got the doggy rule book and they're following it to the letter.

In the other corner, we have the traditionalists. They rely on dominance and punishment – it's like they're still using a rotary phone in the age of smartphones. But in this battle, science-backed training reigns supreme.

The dogs trained with science-backed methods emerge as the shining stars. They respond positively to training sessions, show reduced signs of fear or aggression, and their owners report stronger bonds. It's like they've aced the training exam with flying colors.

On the flip side, the dogs trained using traditional methods struggle. They show inconsistent improvements in behavior, often accompanied by stress and aggression during training. It's like trying to teach an old dog new tricks, but the tricks aren't that great to begin with.

But science doesn't stop at training methods. It delves deeper into the canine mind, revealing remarkable insights. Imagine your dog as a furry genius, pondering the mysteries of the universe (or at least the mysteries of where you hide the treats).

Scientific studies show that dogs are like furry Einstein's, solving complex problems and even understanding human cues. It's like having a little genius by your side, ready to decode your every command.

And when it comes to memory, dogs are like living diaries. They remember events, people, and places like it's a mental scrapbook. It's like they're constantly flipping through the pages of their memories, reliving the good times (and maybe some embarrassing moments).

But here's where it gets even cooler – dogs have emotional intelligence. They're like little therapists, reading our emotions, understanding social hierarchies, and showing empathy. It's like having a furry best friend who always knows when you need a cuddle.

So, how did science unveil all these doggy secrets? Through rigorous studies in ethology and behavioral science, researchers became doggy detectives. They uncovered the genetic, environmental, and social factors that shape a dog's actions. It's like they cracked the code to dog behavior.

But it didn't stop there. Science revolutionized dog training by creating methods rooted in psychology and behavior science. Think of it as personalized training plans tailored to your dog's unique needs. It's like having a personal trainer who understands every quirk and whim.

Now, let me share a little personal story. I once had a dog named Max – a Border Collie with a stubborn streak. Traditional training methods were like talking to a brick wall. But armed with scientific knowledge, I became the Sherlock Holmes of dog training.

I used positive reinforcement, treats, and clicker training. It was like a light bulb moment for Max. Suddenly, he was eager to learn, and our training sessions were like a well-rehearsed play.

Science transformed Max from a stubborn pup to a cooperative companion. It's like turning a grumpy morning person into someone who sings in the shower. Our bond deepened, and life with Max became a joyous adventure.

So, there you have it – science-backed dog training methods. They're like the keys to unlocking your dog's potential. With them, you'll navigate the training journey with confidence, communication, and a whole lot of tail-wagging fun.

Ethical Considerations

Ethical considerations are at the heart of responsible and effective dog training. Science-backed methods in dog training stand out as not only effective but also highly ethical, prioritizing the well-being of our canine companions. Let's take a closer look at the ethical principles that underpin these methods:

1. **Positive Reinforcement**: Imagine learning a new skill, and every time you make progress, you receive praise and rewards. It's motivating and enjoyable, right? Science-backed dog training takes this approach to heart. Good behavior is met with kindness and rewards, creating a positive and fulfilling training experience for dogs. This positive reinforcement not only boosts a dog's motivation but also strengthens the trust between dogs and their owners. It's like building a partnership based on positivity and mutual respect, a core ethical principle.

2. **Avoiding Punishment-Based Methods**: In contrast to positive reinforcement, punishment-based methods involve scolding or physical corrections when a dog makes a mistake. This can lead to fear, anxiety, and stress in dogs, which is both ethically and emotionally detrimental. Science-backed techniques steer clear of such harsh approaches, prioritizing cooperation over coercion. They ensure that training occurs in a compassionate and humane manner, reflecting a deep commitment to the mental and emotional well-being of dogs.

3. **Respecting Mental and Emotional States**: Positive reinforcement is the cornerstone of humane training. It respects a dog's mental and emotional state, fostering cooperation and trust. Dogs thrive in a stress-free environment, and science-backed methods create precisely that – an environment where dogs can learn and thrive while maintaining their emotional health. This ethical approach safeguards a dog's well-being throughout the training process.

Luna's Inspiring Journey

To illustrate the ethical excellence of science-backed training, let's explore the heartwarming journey of Luna, a rescue dog who faced a challenging past marked by neglect and mistreatment, leaving her timid and anxious. Luna's story showcases the profound impact of science-backed methods:

Luna's new owner, Lisa, was determined to help Luna overcome her traumatic experiences. They embarked on a journey guided by science-backed methods, emphasizing core ethical principles such as patience, consistency, and empathy. Luna's transformation began with trust-building exercises, where she learned to trust Lisa and respond to commands with enthusiasm. The training approach was rooted in rewards, praise, and a deep understanding of Luna's unique needs – an ethical recipe for her success.

However, science-backed training went beyond just basic obedience. It empowered Lisa to identify Luna's triggers and address them with empathy and care. Over time, Luna's fears began to fade, replaced by a newfound sense of security. She blossomed into a playful and affectionate companion, showcasing the remarkable resilience of rescue animals when provided with ethical and compassionate training.

Luna's story is a testament to the ethical power of humane, science-backed training. It serves as a vivid reminder that every rescue dog deserves a chance at a brighter future, guided by compassion and effective methods. It's a story of transformation, trust, and the extraordinary bond that can be forged between humans and their four-legged friends when ethics are at the forefront of training – a shining example of how science-backed techniques contribute to the overall well-being of our beloved canine companions.

Debunking Common Myths

I'm sure you've heard the age-old myth that "old dogs can't learn new tricks." It's a phrase that's been tossed around, often accompanied by a resigned shrug. But here's the twist – science-backed research is here to say, "Hold my treat bag!" Let's unravel this myth with a touch of humor and some enlightening insights.

You see, this myth suggests that older dogs are like seasoned professors who've already written their dissertations and have no room for new knowledge. But the truth? Well, it's a bit more dynamic than that. Science dives headfirst into this doggy dilemma, introducing us to the captivating concept of neuroplasticity.

Neuroplasticity, my dear readers, is like a dog's brain doing a tango – it can rewire itself and learn new moves, no matter the age. So, if you've ever caught your senior pup giving you the side-eye during training, rest assured that their mental machinery is still chugging along, ready for action.

But don't just take my word for it. Science has thrown us a bone here. Recent studies have shown that older dogs can indeed pick up new tricks. Yes, you read that correctly – the golden oldies have got it going on when it comes to learning.

Now, let's dive into some delightful tales from the trenches of doggy academia, where our four-legged scholars prove that age is but a number.

Picture this: Charlie, an eleven-year-old Labrador Retriever with a penchant for proving myths wrong. His human, Susan, was initially skeptical – who trains an old dog, right? But Susan was up for the challenge and armed with science-backed wisdom.

Charlie had been a good boy throughout his life, but as the years rolled by, he developed some quirks. Thunderstorms had him shaking like a leaf and barking up a storm. Susan was on a mission to turn this canine thunder-phobia into a thing of the past.

Enter science-backed counter-conditioning – the art of changing emotional responses through positivity. Susan's plan was simple yet brilliant. Whenever thunderclouds gathered, she turned up the tunes (soothing ones, of course), handed Charlie his favorite treats, and engaged in some gentle play. Thunder was no longer just a storm; it was a party!

Now, let me tell you, my friends, the transformation was nothing short of remarkable. Over time, Charlie's anxiety began to fizzle out like a damp firework. Those once-dreaded thunderstorms turned into opportunities for treats and fun. Susan couldn't believe her eyes (or ears, for that matter). Her senior pup had mastered the art of new tricks, proving that science-backed techniques are a timeless treasure.

So, next time someone drops the "old dogs can't learn new tricks" bomb, you can whip out your science-backed knowledge and say, "Well, actually…" Age, it turns out, is just a number in the world of canine wisdom and neuroplasticity.

And of course you know the enduring legend of asserting alpha status in your dog's world. It's like a classic bedtime story, a narrative that once had us thinking we needed a royal scepter to rule our furry pals. But hold your biscuits, because modern science has a fresh take on this age-old tale, and we're about to dig into it with a sprinkle of humor and a heap of knowledge.

So, what's the deal with this "alpha" business? Well, it all started with ideas about wolf pack behavior, which someone decided to apply to domestic dogs. The concept was simple: you needed to assert dominance through might and submission. But here's the plot twist – it's a concept that's been thoroughly debunked by science.

Recent research into wolf packs has shown that they function more like cooperative family units rather than doggy dictatorships. Forget about alpha wolves ruling with an iron paw – it's all about teamwork, communication, and mutual respect. So, trying to establish yourself as the "alpha" with your dog is like insisting on speaking Latin at a modern-day pizza party – outdated and bound to lead to some awkward moments.

Science steps in to offer a more nuanced perspective on canine social structures. Dogs aren't looking for an alpha; they're searching for security, companionship, and a good old-fashioned chat with their human pals. It turns out that positive reinforcement, where dogs are rewarded for good behavior, is not only more effective but also builds trust and strengthens the bond between humans and their furry sidekicks.

Now, let's talk about Rex, the German Shepherd with a story that will have you wagging your tail in delight. His owner, Tom, once believed that being the alpha was the key to canine obedience. Tom dabbled in techniques like alpha rolls and physical corrections, thinking it was the royal road to a well-behaved pup.

But here's where the plot thickens. Rex, despite Tom's best intentions, began to feel more like a prisoner than a partner. Anxiety and aggression crept in, casting a shadow over their once-happy companionship. Tom knew something had to change, and change it did!

Tom swapped his alpha crown for a science-backed approach. He embraced positive reinforcement, rewarding Rex for good behavior and using clear, friendly commands. The transformation was nothing short of magical. Rex became an eager student in their training sessions, and his anxiety? Well, it packed its bags and left town. Their relationship blossomed, with Rex no longer fearing Tom but respecting him as a friend.

This tale of Rex is a shining example that dogs don't thrive on dominance-based training. Instead, they respond to kindness, respect, and clear communication. Rex's journey showcases how ditching the alpha act in favor of science-backed methods leads to better behavior, improved relationships, and happier, well-adjusted dogs. So, next time someone says you need to be the alpha, you can tell them, "Science says we're better off being the best pals!"

Positive reinforcement in dog training is like setting up the ultimate doggy game show – "The Good Behavior Challenge." In this imaginary canine game show, your pup doesn't get to host their own program; instead, they become the star contestant competing for treats, praise, and the coveted title of "Best Behaved Woofer." You, on the other hand, are the charismatic game show host, enthusiastically laying out the rules and generously rewarding those winning behaviors like they just won the canine lottery.

Imagine your home as the elaborate game show set, complete with props, cues, and scripts. Jim, Bella's owner, takes on the role of the director and scriptwriter, crafting a story-line where Bella learns the art of polite guest greetings and the value of serene walks.

The curtain rises on Bella's first scene: the infamous guest-jumping routine. It used to be a performance that put her on center stage, but Jim had other plans. Armed with treats and boundless patience, he directed Bella to sit politely and extend a paw of welcome instead. With each successful take, treats rained down like confetti at a championship game. Bella quickly grasped her role, and guest greetings turned from chaotic to charming.

Next came the bark-o-rama scene. Instead of ear-splitting barking, Bella was now a maestro of quieter, melodious woofs. Jim had introduced a cue, "Hush," which Bella obeyed with precision. The audience (which includes Bella herself) applauded her new-found vocal finesse with treats, scratches, and lots of praise.

Then, there were the leisurely strolls – the final act of the show. Bella had once pulled Jim like a determined sled dog, but now, with the magic of positive reinforcement, she walked like a dignified royalty on a victory parade. Treats and praises flowed freely as Bella mastered the art of loose leash walking.

So, think of it this way – positive reinforcement is the blockbuster hit that turns your wild pup into a well-behaved celebrity, all while you get to play the role of the proud, treat-dispensing director. Science-backed training techniques: bringing out the best in dogs, making life a real-life sitcom filled with laughter and tail wags, and ensuring that both you and your four-legged companion enjoy every moment of the show, from the opening act to the final bow.

Getting the Best Results

Importance of Consistency

Consistency in dog training is like the secret ingredient in your grandma's famous cake recipe – it's the unsung hero that makes the whole thing work. Imagine if Grandma decided to swap sugar with salt and flour with, say, sawdust every now and then. You'd end up with some pretty unpredictable cakes, right? Well, the same goes for dog training – consistency is the secret sauce that ensures your pup turns into a well-behaved, non-sawdust-eating furry friend.

Now, let's break down what consistency is all about in doggy boot camp. First off, it's like having a choreographed dance routine. You can't have one dancer doing the cha-cha while another does the moonwalk – that's just chaos. Likewise, in dog training, the commands should be like synchronized dance moves. No ad-libbing allowed!

Then there are the rewards – the doggy version of getting paid in treats, belly rubs, and playtime. Imagine if you were a kid doing chores for your allowance, but sometimes you got a crisp $20 bill, other times a pat on the back, and occasionally a shiny new toy. You'd be utterly confused, right? Well, so would your dog. Consistency here means the same rewards, at the same time, for the same awesome behaviors.

Now, think of consistency like your dog's personal Netflix binge-watching schedule. Imagine if one day they get to watch their favorite show at 7 PM, and the next day it's at 3 AM – they'd be bewildered. Dogs thrive on routines, just like you do with your evening popcorn and Netflix ritual.

Okay, enough of the cake, dancing, and Netflix metaphors. Let's get to the real-life stories, like the tale of Tracy, the high-energy Labrador. David, her owner, decided to ditch the chaos and embrace consistency. He turned into the "Captain Consistency" of dog training. Clear commands, consistent rewards, and a daily schedule that could rival a Swiss watch – that was David's new plan. And guess what? Tracy went from being the class clown to the teacher's pet. Well, not literally, but you get the idea.

The Science Behind Consistency

Now, let's talk science. Did you know that dogs are memory champs? They remember where you keep their treats, the exact spot they buried their favorite bone last summer, and even that one time you accidentally dropped a piece of cheese. Consistency taps into this memory superpower. It's like hitting the "Save" button on a computer game after a particularly successful level – it reinforces the behavior.

Consistent positive reinforcement is like building a bridge between good behavior and delicious treats. The more you reinforce it consistently, the stronger that bridge becomes.

And here's the fun part – dogs are like creatures of habit. When they know there's a tasty treat waiting for them every time they do something right, they'll turn into little behavior enthusiasts. It's like convincing a kid that broccoli is the secret to becoming a superhero – they'll do it happily if it means a reward at the end.

Consistency Across Caregivers

But wait, there's more! Consistency isn't a one-person show; it's a family affair. Picture this: you're in a band, and each member plays a different tune on their own instrument. You'd end up with a noise that not even your dog would appreciate. In the world of dog training, every family member should play the same harmonious tune.

Commands and actions should be like a family recipe passed down through generations – everyone follows the same steps. Imagine if Dad says "Sit" while Mom says "Plonk your bottom" – the dog might be left thinking they've been teleported to a comedy show!

And it's not just about commands; it's also about rules, boundaries, and routines. Consistency in the household is like having a script for your family sitcom – everyone knows their lines, the plot makes sense, and the audience (including your dog) loves every episode.

In the Smith family, they knew this all too well. With their dog Troy, they realized that consistency was the key to doggy success. They held family meetings, agreed on the rules, and practiced synchronized commands. Troy went from being a canine chaos conductor to a well-behaved family member who was no longer plotting the great sock heist.

In conclusion, consistency is like the secret recipe that turns your dog into the star of their own blockbuster movie. It's grounded in science, it's a family effort, and it's the reason your dog's tail wags happily in every scene of their training journey. So remember, when it comes to dog training, consistency isn't just a cherry on top – it's the whole darn sundae.

Role of Timing

Timing of Rewards

Let's not forget the mystical art of reward timing in dog training – it's like catching a shooting star; you've got to be quick and precise! You see, timing isn't just about handing out treats; it's about making your dog feel like they've won the lottery every time they nail a trick. It's the canine version of hitting the jackpot in Vegas.

Trainers swear by the "three-second rule." No, it's not a rule for picking up dropped food – it's the golden law of giving rewards within three seconds of a job well done. Why, you ask? Because dogs have the attention span of a squirrel on a caffeine rush. They need instant feedback to connect the dots between their behavior and the tasty prize.

Think about it like this: You tell your dog to sit, and they plop their bottom down like they've just won a game show. If you take too long to deliver that treat, they might think they've won the lottery, changed their name to Sir Sit-a-Lot, and saved the world from a biscuit shortage, all before you even said "Good boy!"

Now, let's talk about delay – not the kind that happens when your dog decides to take an eternity to sniff a lamppost. Delaying rewards is like telling your dog, "Remember that thing you did two hours ago? Here's a treat for it." Confusion galore! They're left scratching their heads, wondering if they've slipped into a time warp where treats rain from the sky at random intervals.

Arthur, our dog training wizard, had the timing skills of a ninja. His dogs practically teleported into good behavior because he followed the

25

three-second rule religiously. Immediate praise and treats created a mental link between actions and rewards faster than you can say "Fetch!"

Timing of Corrections

Now, let's venture into the world of corrections – the doggy version of getting caught with your hand in the cookie jar. Just like with rewards, timing here is crucial for setting the record straight.

Picture this: your dog decides to redecorate the living room with some creative digging. You can't wait until next week to say, "Hey, that wasn't a home improvement project!" Nope, you've got to deliver that correction immediately, like a director yelling "Cut!" in the middle of a scene gone wrong.

Prompt corrections provide clarity for dogs. They're like traffic signs that say, "Dead end – don't go this way!" Delayed corrections, on the other hand, are like putting up the sign after the dog has already taken a detour. They'll be left wondering why you've decided to decorate the living room with a "No Digging" sign.

Let's dive into another scenario: jumping up on guests. If you correct this behavior minutes later, your dog will think you're upset about something else entirely – like their plans to audition for a canine dance-off.

Buddy, the bouncing Beagle, knew the power of prompt corrections. His owner had ninja-like timing skills when it came to correcting undesirable behavior. Buddy quickly learned the house rules and became the model house guest.

Timing in Training Sessions

Now, let's talk about the length of those training sessions. Remember, dogs have the attention span of a squirrel, so think of training sessions like short, thrilling episodes of their favorite TV show – engaging and over before you can say "commercial break."

Sessions should typically last around 10 to 15 minutes – just enough time to keep your pup's interest without turning them into a canine couch potato. When your dog starts staring off into the distance or planning their next squirrel chase, it's time to wrap things up.

Samantha, the savvy dog owner, went from marathon training sessions to bite-sized, action-packed ones. Her dog, Rocky, went from "Wait, what are we doing again?" to "I'm ready for my close-up, Mr. DeMille!" Shorter sessions meant Rocky had more energy, enthusiasm, and a better memory than a computer with extra RAM.

Rusty, the unruly Bulldog, had his transformation moment too. Consistency and well-timed rewards and corrections, paired with short, engaging training sessions, turned him from a walking chaos machine into a doggy Einstein.

In conclusion, timing in dog training is like playing a symphony – every note, every pause, and every crescendo matters. Adhering to the "three-second rule" for rewards and offering immediate feedback for corrections is like conducting a masterpiece. And keeping training sessions short and sweet? Well, that's like hitting all the high notes in your dog's training journey, turning them into the well-behaved, happy stars they were born to be.

"Next, let's build on this foundation by diving into basic commands."

2

Mastering Basic Commands in 10 Minutes

"Mastering the basics is not just about obedience; it's the cornerstone of communication between you and your dog."
— Ian Dunbar, Veterinarian, Animal Behaviorist, and Dog Trainer.

* * *

Dash, my border collie rescue, is delightfully a handful. Eager to explore, he'd bolt at any chance. Obedience training was a necessity. We began with basic commands like 'Sit' and 'Stay,' which required patience and consistent practice. Slowly, he mastered them. 'Come' was a game-changer; teaching it took persistence, but it was worth every effort. One day, while hiking, Dash spotted a rabbit and took off. Heart in my throat, I yelled, "Come!" He returned, muddy but unharmed, proving that obedience saved him from harm. Dash's journey in mastering commands was a testament to dedication, trust, and a bond that kept him safe.

Understanding Basic Commands

Why Start with Basics?

The basics of dog training - where all the fun begins! Starting with the fundamentals is like laying the first brick in the doggy house of obedience. But why should we bother with the basics, you ask? Well, besides impressing your friends with your dog's impeccable manners, it's all about safety and sanity, for both you and your furry friend.

Imagine this: you're on a leisurely stroll in the park, and suddenly, your dog spots a squirrel on a mission. Without the basics like "stop" and "come," you're in for a wild ride, my friend. Mastering the basics is like giving your dog a universal remote control to navigate life's adventures. Commands like "sit," "stay," and "come" are your secret weapons to prevent your pup from turning your walk into a squirrel-chasing marathon.

But it's not just about avoiding parkour-style squirrel encounters. These basics build the foundation for a beautiful dog-owner friendship. Picture this: you're at the dog park, and your pup is making new furry pals. But when it's time to head home, a simple "come" command can save you from a game of hide-and-seek with your Houdini hound.

Now, let's talk about the benefits of mastering the basics, shall we? Immediate obedience means you have a well-behaved co-pilot for life's journey. These basics are like your dog's GPS for good behavior, guiding them through everyday situations. And guess what? It gets even better!

Once your dog conquers the basics, they're ready to level up in the obedience game. It's like going from basic math to advanced calculus (well, maybe not that complicated, but you get the idea). With the basics firmly under their furry belt, learning advanced commands becomes a breeze. Positive reinforcement is your trusty sidekick in this training adventure, keeping your dog motivated and tail-waggingly happy.

Dogs, like humans, have a learning curve that varies with age. Puppies are like sponges, soaking up knowledge faster than a thirsty camel in the desert. Adolescents might be a bit scatterbrained, but they're up for a challenge. Adults are steady learners, while seniors might need a bit more patience.

Starting with the basics aligns perfectly with your dog's brainpower at different stages of life. It's like giving them the right puzzle pieces for their cognitive development. Simple commands, like "sit" and "stay," are like the beginner's level in a video game - they boost your dog's confidence and set the stage for tackling more complex tasks.

So, there you have it, the science-backed wisdom of starting with the basics. It's not just about teaching your dog manners; it's about building a strong foundation for a lifelong partnership. Plus, who doesn't want a dog that can impress with tricks beyond just rolling over and playing dead? So, grab those treats, put on your training hat, and get ready for a journey of canine enlightenment!

A story of a dog who mastered advanced tricks only after solidifying basic commands

Let me introduce you to Max, the canine virtuoso, or so he became. Max started his training journey with the grace of a bull in a china shop. Basic commands like "sit" and "stay" were about as foreign to him as rocket science is to most of us. It was a comical sight, really, watching Max's attempts at obedience resemble a dance routine gone hilariously wrong.

But here's where the magic happened. Max's owner, let's call her Sarah, didn't throw in the leash and give up. No, Sarah was determined to help Max unleash his inner genius. So, she rolled up her sleeves, dusted off the training treats, and got to work.

With unwavering patience and a stash of treats that could rival a candy store, Sarah drilled the basics into Max's brain. "Sit" became a moment of triumph rather than confusion. "Stay" transformed from a head-tilting mystery into a skillful pause. It was like watching a bumbling apprentice become a master of his craft.

But here's where the plot thickens, folks. Once Max had the basics down pat, he set his sights on more advanced tricks. It was like he had discovered a treasure trove of canine knowledge and couldn't wait to unlock its secrets. Suddenly, "roll over" became a graceful tumble, "play dead" was a dramatic masterpiece, and "fetch the newspaper" turned into a daily delivery service.

Max didn't stop there, oh no. He ventured into the world of agility courses, leaping over hurdles and weaving through poles with the finesse of an Olympic gymnast. He even became a pro at responding to emergency cues like "lie down" and "Stop and Stand," proving that a solid foundation can unlock a world of possibilities.

Max's transformation was nothing short of spectacular. He went from a disobedient goofball to a canine Einstein, all thanks to Sarah's dedication to mastering the basics. Max's story reminds us that every dog has the potential for greatness, and it all begins with a strong foundation. So, the next time you're teaching your pup to sit, remember, you might just be setting the stage for a future four-legged genius!

Now that you've heard Max's tale of triumph, let's delve deeper into why mastering basic commands is the paw-some key to unlocking your dog's full potential.

● Safety First!

Picture this: you're out for a leisurely stroll with your furry friend when you spot a squirrel in the distance. Your dog's ears perk up, and that mischievous glint appears in their eyes. Without missing a beat, you command, "Stay!" And just like that, your pup remains firmly rooted, squirrel-chasing ambitions thwarted.

Basic commands like "stay" and "come" aren't just handy party tricks; they're a lifeline in unexpected situations. They can prevent your dog from darting into traffic, chasing wildlife, or getting into other sticky situations. It's like having a remote control for your dog's safety.

● Harmony at Home

Life with a well-trained dog is like a symphony where every note is in perfect harmony. Imagine hosting a dinner party with your impeccably behaved canine companion by your side. As your guests marvel at your dog's good manners, you'll be beaming with pride.

Basic commands lay the groundwork for a harmonious coexistence. "Sit" keeps your dog from leaping onto your guests, "stay" ensures they don't steal snacks from the table, and "quiet" saves you from a cacophony of barking during your favorite TV show.

● Stress-Free Adventures

Adventures with your dog are the stuff of memories, but they can quickly turn into nightmares without basic commands. Picture a hike through the woods with your furry explorer. With a firm "come" command, your dog returns from chasing a butterfly, allowing you to continue your trek without a hitch.

Basic commands are your passport to stress-free adventures. Whether you're hiking, traveling, or simply enjoying a day at the park, knowing that your dog will respond to your cues ensures a worry-free experience.

● Building Trust and Bonding

Trust is the glue that holds any relationship together, including the one you share with your four-legged friend. When your dog understands and obeys your commands, it builds trust like nothing else.

Think about it—when your dog looks up at you with those soulful eyes and follows your guidance, it's a heartwarming moment of connection. You become their leader, their confidant, their partner in crime (the good kind, of course

The 'Sit' Command

Now that we've established the importance of basic commands, let's dive into the classic "Sit" command. It's like teaching your dog proper manners at the canine dinner table, and it's often the first step in their education.

Why it's generally the first command taught

The "Sit" command has a front-row seat in the doggie classroom for several reasons, and it's not just because it's a dog's way of saying "please." Here's why it's the headliner of canine education:

Firstly, it's a fundamental and practical command that establishes a basis for more advanced training. Teaching a dog to sit helps build a strong communication foundation between the owner and the dog. Think of it as the canine version of learning the ABCs before tackling Shakespeare.

Secondly, sitting is a natural and non-threatening behavior for dogs, making it relatively easy to teach. Dogs don't need a degree in canine calculus to understand this one. This early success boosts the dog's confidence, which is essential for any aspiring scholar. Imagine if you had to start your education with advanced quantum physics; you'd be feeling a bit overwhelmed too!

Tips for successful "sit" training

Now, let's roll up our sleeves (or should I say, roll over our paws) and get into the nitty-gritty of teaching your dog this quintessential command. Here's a step-by-step guide that even a canine scholar can appreciate:

1. Prepare Treats: Gather some small, tasty treats that your dog loves. Think of these treats as the doggie equivalent of gold stars.
2. Choose a Quiet Location: Find a quiet, distraction-free area to train your dog. It's like creating a library for focused learning.
3. Get Your Dog's Attention: Call your dog by its name to get its attention. Use a happy and encouraging tone; after all, enthusiasm is contagious!

4. Hold a Treat: Now, it's time for the magic wand—a treat! Hold it close to your dog's nose so they can catch a whiff of what's in store.

5. Lure the Sit: Slowly move the treat from their nose upwards and slightly back over their head. Your dog's nose will follow the treat, and their butt should lower naturally as they try to keep an eye on the treat. It's like a canine limbo dance, but instead of going under a pole, they're going down!

6. Say "Sit": As your dog's butt touches the ground, say "sit" in a clear and firm voice. Timing is crucial, so say it as their rear end hits the ground. Think of it as awarding them the "Sit of Approval" in real-time.

7. Reward and Praise: As soon as your dog sits, give them the treat immediately and offer verbal praise like "Good sit!" or "Well done!" It's like giving them a standing ovation for their impeccable sitting skills.

8. Repeat: Practice this multiple times in a short training session. Keep it positive and fun; after all, who doesn't love a good treat-earning session?

9. Add Duration: Once your dog reliably sits when you say "sit," start increasing the duration before giving the treat. For example, wait a few seconds before rewarding. It's like moving from short essays to full-length novels in the canine school of literature.

10. Practice Regularly: Consistency is key, just like practicing your favorite dance moves. Practice the "sit" command daily for short sessions.

11. Use "Sit" in Real Life: Start using the "sit" command in real-life situations, like before feeding, going outside, or when guests arrive. It's like applying what you learned in school to real-world situations.

12. Gradually Reduce Treats: Over time, reduce the frequency of

treats but continue to praise and reward your dog occasionally to reinforce the behavior. Think of it as transitioning from gold stars to verbal praise as your dog becomes a seasoned "sit" pro.

13. Proof the Command: Practice "sit" in various environments and with different people to make sure your dog understands and obeys the command in different situations. It's like taking your show on the road and proving you can dance anywhere, anytime.

Remember that all dogs learn at their own pace, so be patient and positive throughout the training process. If your dog is struggling, seek professional training help if necessary or feel free to reach out to me using the contact page at www.BorderColliePassion.com.

Common mistakes and how to avoid them

Now, let's address some common hiccups in the "sit" command journey and how to sidestep them:

One common mistake is being inconsistent with the command. If you use multiple words or phrases to signal the same action, your dog may become confused. It's like trying to learn multiple languages at once; it can get quite perplexing. Stick to a single, clear cue like "sit" to ensure your dog understands what's expected, and they won't need a translator.

Another common error is impatience. Dogs may not grasp the command immediately, and becoming impatient or frustrated can hinder the training process. It's like expecting a first-time chef to whip up a gourmet meal on their debut. It's crucial to stay calm, maintain a positive attitude, and reward even small improvements. Consistency is key; repeating the command numerous times or neglecting to reward can be detrimental. Your dog may learn to ignore the command if it doesn't result in a reward.

Using physical force or negative reinforcement is a significant mistake. Forcing your dog into a sitting position or scolding them for not sitting can create anxiety and undermine trust. It's like trying to learn to dance while someone is constantly pushing you around; not fun at all. Instead, use positive reinforcement techniques, such as treats and praise, to encourage your dog to follow the command willingly. It's essential to maintain a supportive and nurturing environment during the training process to achieve the best results.

So, there you have it, the "Sit" command decoded with a dash of humor and a sprinkle of wisdom. Now you and your furry friend can embark on a journey of obedience, trust, and impeccable manners, one sit at a time!

The 'Stay' Command

Importance in safety scenarios

'Stay' command, which is like your dog's secret recipe for mastering the art of patience and safety. This command isn't just about making your furry friend do the doggie version of a freeze frame; it's a vital skill for keeping them safe in various situations.

Picture this: You're on a leisurely stroll with your dog, and suddenly a squirrel dashes across the path. Without the 'Stay' command, your dog might go from zero to a hundred in seconds, darting off like a furry rocket. That's where the magic of 'Stay' comes in. It's like an emergency brake for your dog, ensuring they don't turn a leisurely walk into a wild chase scene.

The 'Stay' command is vital for ensuring your dog's safety in various situations. It prevents them from running into traffic, approaching dangerous wildlife, or engaging with potentially aggressive dogs. It also helps in everyday situations like keeping your dog from bolting out the front door. In short, 'Stay' is your canine lifesaver.

Step-by-step guide to teaching 'stay'

Now, let's unwrap the mystery of teaching your dog this life-saving command. But before diving into 'Stay,' make sure your dog has aced the basics like 'sit' and 'lie down.' With that prerequisite checked, here's a 13-step guide to training your dog in the art of 'Stay':

1. Choose a Quiet Location: Start your training in a quiet area with minimal distractions. Think of it as creating a serene Zen garden for doggie wisdom.
2. Gather Treats: As always, keep those tantalizing treats at the ready. These will be your secret weapon.
3. Begin with "Sit": Before 'Stay,' there's 'Sit.' Make sure your dog is comfortable with this command.
4. Get Your Dog's Attention: Call your dog's name to capture their focus. Think of it as ringing the bell to start class.
5. Use a Leash (optional): If your dog is new to training, a leash can be your trusty ally in keeping them close.
6. Give the "Sit" Command: Ask your dog to sit. It's like instructing them to take a seat in the classroom of life.
7. Open Your Hand: Extend your hand, palm facing your dog, and say "Stay" as you take a step back. It's like saying, "Stay, my dear Watson!"
8. Reward and Praise: If your dog remains in the sitting position, return to them and reward with a treat and praise. It's like handing

them a gold star for their patience.

9. Increase Distance Gradually: Take a step back, then another, and gradually increase the distance over several training sessions. Think of it as your dog earning their 'Stay' diploma one step at a time.

10. Use Hand Signal: To add a touch of flair, introduce a hand signal, like an open palm facing your dog, as a visual cue for "stay." It's like teaching them sign language for dogs.

11. Duration: Gradually increase the time your dog must stay in place before receiving the treat. It's like challenging them to a game of 'Stay' endurance.

12. Practice with Distractions: Introduce controlled distractions to test your dog's ability to stay in different situations. It's like adding plot twists to their training story.

13. Release Command: Teach a release command, like "OK" or "Free," to let your dog know when they can move. It's like saying, "You're free to go, my furry friend!"

Remember that consistency, patience, and positive reinforcement are your trusty companions when teaching the "Stay" command. Some dogs may take longer to master this art of patience than others, so go at your dog's pace and make training sessions enjoyable.

Challenges and how to overcome them

Let's address some of the challenges you might encounter while teaching 'Stay,' and how to tackle them like a pro:

One common challenge is a lack of focus. Dogs can easily become distracted, especially in new or stimulating environments. It's like trying to meditate in a noisy, crowded room. To overcome this, start training in a quiet, controlled space, and gradually introduce distractions as your dog becomes more proficient. It's like moving from beginner to advanced meditation levels.

Another hurdle is impatience, both on the part of the owner and the dog. Training can be frustrating, but remember, it's a journey, not a race. Keep training sessions short and enjoyable, and never use punishment, as it can lead to fear and resistance. Consistency is vital; repeating the command numerous times or neglecting to reward can be detrimental. Your dog may learn to ignore the command if it doesn't result in a reward. It's like trying to motivate someone with empty promises; it won't work.

Lastly, boredom can be a tough nut to crack. Dogs, like humans, can become disinterested if training becomes monotonous. It's like attending a lecture with no enthusiasm. To tackle this, make sessions fun and varied, using a mix of treats, toys, and praise to keep your dog motivated. Adapting to your dog's learning style is crucial; some respond better to visual cues, while others favor verbal commands. Pay attention to what works best for your specific dog. Always remember that every dog is unique and may learn at their own pace. Stay patient, and if you're facing significant challenges, consider seeking guidance from a professional dog trainer.

With 'Stay' in their repertoire, your dog will be the picture of patience and safety, ready to face any adventure with poise and obedience. So, embrace the art of 'Stay' and watch your dog become a Zen master of patience and obedience!

Adding visual cues to your verbal commands is a vital aspect of effective dog training, especially as our furry friends age and their hearing abilities may decline. While verbal cues can significantly enhance communication with your dog, there's no denying that visual cues also play a pivotal role. As dogs grow older, their hearing may become less sharp, making visual cues invaluable in conveying your expectations. However, it's essential to remember that dogs don't always have their eyes trained on us, making verbal cues a crucial safety net. Imagine a scenario where your senior dog is exploring the yard, and you spot a potential danger approaching – a speeding car or another hazard. A well-timed verbal or other auditory command can swiftly grab their attention and avert a potentially dangerous situation, ensuring their safety even when their focus is elsewhere.

As my 15 year old Border Collie, Gadget, is aging, she is almost completely deaf to voices. We have incorporated a clap of the hands to get her attention turned to us, and then we use our visual cues to let her know what we want from her.

In essence, the combination of visual and verbal cues creates a comprehensive communication system that can adapt to your dog's changing needs, enhancing their overall well-being and safety as they age, but we'll talk more about this a bit later.

The 'Come' Command

Why it's a life-saving command

The "Come" command, the superhero of dog training commands, coming to the rescue when you need your furry sidekick to return promptly. It's not just a command; it's a lifesaver, and here's why.

Why it's a life-saving command

Imagine this: Your dog, caught up in a whirlwind of excitement, is sprinting towards a busy road. Panic sets in, but then you utter those magical words, "Come here!" Your dog's ears perk up, and they make a beeline for you, averting disaster. That's the magic of the "Come" command – it's your lifeline in critical moments.

The "Come" command is life-saving because it allows you to regain control of your dog in various situations. Whether your dog is about to run into traffic, approach an aggressive animal, or needs to be brought back on a leash, a reliable recall can prevent accidents and ensure your dog's safety. It's like having a remote control to summon your dog back to your side when danger lurks.

Techniques for teaching effective recall

Let's dive into the art of teaching your dog this incredible recall command. It's your dog's version of being called to the stage, and they'll eagerly respond with a standing ovation. Here are 15 steps to help you achieve this feat:

1. Start Indoors: Begin your dog's recall education in a quiet, indoor environment to minimize distractions. Think of it as teaching them the basics before the grand performance.
2. Choose a Special Recall Word: Pick a unique word or phrase for the recall command, such as "come" or "here." This word will be music to your dog's ears.
3. Use Positive Reinforcement: Arm yourself with plenty of high-value treats or toys as rewards. It's like bribing them with doggie gold!
4. Leash Training: If your dog is not leash trained, start by introduc-

ing them to a leash indoors. It's like handing them a backstage pass to the world of recall.

5. Practice Indoors: Call your dog using the recall word and gently pull on the leash to guide them towards you. It's the opening act of the recall show.

6. Reward and Praise: When your dog heeds your call and trots over, shower them with a treat and lots of praise. It's the standing ovation they deserve.

7. Consistency: Use the same recall word each time and be consistent with your gestures. Think of it as sticking to the script.

8. Gradual Distractions: As your dog gets better at recalling indoors, introduce a few more distractions, like a squeaky toy or a friendly neighborhood squirrel.

9. Outdoor Training: Take your recall training outdoors, but make sure it's in a secure, fenced area. Think of it as moving to a bigger stage.

10. Short Leash: Start with a short leash to maintain control. It's like keeping your dog on a tight leash during rehearsals.

11. Gradual Off-Leash Training: When your dog consistently recalls on the short leash, gradually increase the distance and switch to a long line. It's like giving them a little more freedom on stage.

12. Positive Associations: Ensure that coming to you is always a positive experience by offering rewards and praise. It's like giving them a standing ovation every time.

13. Avoid Punishment: Remember, even if your dog takes a while to respond, never scold or punish them when they finally come to you. Punishment can make them associate "Come" with negativity, and that's a real showstopper.

14. Random Reinforcement: Occasionally surprise your dog with treats or play, but not every time they come. It's like throwing in some unexpected plot twists to keep them engaged.

15. Real-Life Practice: Practice recall in various outdoor settings with increasing distractions to ensure reliable results. It's like taking your dog on a world tour of recall success.

Effective recall training requires patience and consistency. Keep training sessions positive and enjoyable for your dog, and remember that mastering recall takes time and practice. Always prioritize safety, particularly when transitioning to off-leash training, by doing so in a controlled environment.

Troubleshooting when your dog doesn't respond

Now, let's troubleshoot like pros when your dog seems to be in a different world, ignoring your call. Here are some tips:

Ensure you have high-value treats or rewards to motivate your dog. Sometimes, a more exciting reward can make a difference. It's like offering your dog backstage passes to their favorite concert. Never scold or punish your dog when they finally decide to respond, even if it took them a while. Remember, in the recall show, the important thing is the grand finale, not how long it takes to get there. If your dog constantly ignores the command, consider going back to basic training in a controlled environment, like a rehearsal before the big performance. Gradually increase distractions as they regain their recall confidence.

The 'Heel' Command

The "heel" command, the doggy version of a synchronized dance routine, but with more tail wags and fewer cha-cha-chas. It's the art of walking side by side, and it's not just a fancy maneuver; it's incredibly beneficial for your daily strolls.

Why 'heel' is beneficial for walks

The "heel" command is a fundamental component of dog training, particularly for walks. When a dog heels, it walks closely beside its owner, usually on the left side. This position promotes a sense of order and discipline during walks, ensuring that the dog doesn't pull on the leash or lead the way. It's like teaching your dog to be the perfect dance partner on the sidewalk.

Heeling enhances the safety of both the dog and the owner by preventing tugging on the leash, lunging, or sudden erratic movements. It's a way to establish control and cooperation between the dog and its handler. Think of it as a well-choreographed routine where you and your dog move in harmony, and the sidewalk is your dance floor.

Methods for training your dog to heel

Let's dive into the steps of teaching your dog this dance of obedience, the "heel." It's like preparing for a doggy ballroom competition:

1. Start with Basic Obedience: Before your dog can waltz into heeling, make sure they have mastered basic commands like "sit," "stay," and "come." It's like ensuring they have the right dance moves before the big performance.
2. Choose the Right Equipment: Just like a dancer needs the right shoes, your dog needs the right equipment. Use a well-fitting harness or collar and a standard leash. A front-clip harness or head collar can be your dog's dance attire for better control and

redirection.

3. Select a Quiet Training Area: Begin your dance lessons in a quiet, low-distraction area. It's like practicing your dance routine in a serene studio before hitting the grand stage.

4. Use a Marker Word: Choose your dance command, like "heel" or "close," and stick to it. It's like having a signature move in your routine.

5. Position Your Dog: Start with your dog on your preferred side (usually left) and the leash in your right hand. Hold the leash with a little slack and your arm relaxed. Imagine you're leading your partner onto the dance floor.

6. Start Walking: Begin your dance routine, and as soon as your dog starts to pull or move ahead, gently say the marker word (e.g., "heel") and immediately change direction. It's like executing a perfect twirl on the dance floor.

7. Reward the Right Position: When your dog gracefully returns to your side and walks without pulling, praise them and offer treats. Positive reinforcement is your standing ovation.

8. Maintain Consistency: Continue dancing, repeating the routine whenever your dog tries to steal the spotlight by getting ahead or pulling. Be consistent with your cues and rewards.

9. Gradually Increase Distractions: Just like a dance routine gets more challenging with added elements, practice heeling in areas with more distractions, such as parks or near other dogs.

10. Use Variable Rewards: While initially, you may reward frequently, gradually transition to intermittent rewards to keep the dance exciting. It's like throwing in some surprise moves to keep your partner engaged.

11. Practice Regularly: Consistency is key to perfecting any dance routine. Short, frequent training sessions are more effective than long, infrequent ones.

12. Be Patient and Positive: Stay patient and maintain a positive attitude during training. Your dog will learn at its own pace, and every dance partner is unique.
13. End on a Positive Note: Always end your dance sessions on a positive note, with your dog gracefully heeling and receiving rewards and praise. It's like taking a final bow after a spectacular performance.

Remember that some dogs may take longer to learn to heel, so adjust the tempo to your dog's abilities and temperament. If you're struggling with training, consider seeking help from a professional dog trainer.

Differences between 'heel' and 'follow'

"Heel" and "follow" may sound similar, but they're not the same.

"Heel" is a specific command for walking by your side, like a perfectly coordinated dance duo. It's all about maintaining that elegant posture on the sidewalk.

On the other hand, "follow" is a more general directive for your dog to stay close but not necessarily at your side. It's like giving your dance partner a little more room to groove while still staying connected. "Heel" is commonly used for leash training and obedience, while "follow" allows for more freedom in your dog's movements.

Mastering the "heel" command can turn your daily walks into a graceful dance routine, making them enjoyable and safe for both you and your four-legged dance partner. So, put on your dancing shoes, or rather, your dog's leash, and let the heeling dance begin.

The 'Leave It' Command

The "Leave It" command – it's like the superhero of dog training, swooping in to save the day and protect your furry friend from dangerous items or situations. You know, like when your dog is about to ingest something that's definitely not on the menu.

Protecting your dog from dangerous items

Imagine: Your dog is on a mission to explore the world with their nose, and they stumble upon something that looks oddly appetizing – maybe it's a mysterious object from the sidewalk, a piece of discarded gum, or even a questionable bug. This is where the "Leave It" command comes to the rescue, ensuring your dog doesn't turn into a culinary daredevil.

The "Leave It" command is your dog's shield against potential hazards. It's the ultimate "nope, not today" when it comes to unsafe items or situations. Think of it as your dog's way of saying, "I might be curious, but I value my well-being more than that discarded sandwich."

Steps for teaching 'leave it'

Now, let's unveil the secret to teaching your dog this superhero-level command. Here's how to train your pup to be a "Leave It" expert:

1. Gather Treats: Every superhero needs their reward, right? So, have a stash of treats your dog adores and find a quiet, distraction-free training area to kick off the mission.
2. Hold a Treat in Your Closed Fist: Show your dog a treat – the forbidden fruit – and then dramatically close it in your fist. Your

dog's curiosity will surely kick in.

3. Say "Leave It": In your best superhero voice, utter "leave it" firmly and consistently as you shield the treat with your closed fist. Think of yourself as the doggy Avenger.

4. Wait for the Dog's Reaction: Your dog may paw, sniff, or try to outwit your closed fist. This is the moment of truth. Be patient, for the superhero always waits for the right moment.

5. Wait for a Pause: As soon as your dog momentarily abandons their pursuit of the hidden treasure (even if just for a second), unleash your superhero powers and reward them with a different treat from your other hand. This reinforces that "leave it" equals tasty rewards.

6. Practice: Repeat this heroic exercise, gradually increasing the duration your dog must resist temptation before receiving their reward. You can also level up the challenge by placing the treat on the floor, covering it with your hand, or using a dog-friendly item like a toy instead.

7. Add Distractions: To truly become a "Leave It" superhero, practice with different items and in different locations. Your dog needs to be ready for any mission.

8. Gradually Decrease Rewards: Over time, reduce the frequency of treats but never skimp on the praise and rewards for your furry crime-fighter.

9. Use "Leave It" in Real-Life Situations: Take your superhero skills to the streets – use the "leave it" command when your dog tries to snatch something off the ground during your daily walk. It's like stopping a heist in progress.

10. Consistency and Patience: As with any superhero training, consistency is key. Use the same command and remain patient with your dog's progress. Remember, they're learning a skill that could save the day.

Relevance in advanced training scenarios

But wait, there's more! The "Leave It" command isn't just about averting culinary catastrophes. It's also a valuable tool in advanced training scenarios. Imagine your dog navigating an agility course or mastering off-leash control like a seasoned secret agent. "Leave It" is the ultimate test of impulse control and responsiveness, turning your dog into a well-trained and obedient sidekick.

So, equip your dog with the "Leave It" superpower and watch them become the ultimate protector of their own well-being. It's training that's safe, effective, and ready to save the day – one discarded sandwich at a time!

The 'Lie Down' or 'Down' Command

The "Stay" command – it's like hitting pause on your dog's energetic antics. This command has situational advantages that can save the day, whether you want your dog to remain still while you answer the door or pose for that perfect Instagram-worthy photo.

Situational advantages of the 'stay' command Picture this: You're about to take a family photo with your dog and you want everyone to look picture-perfect. Without the "stay" command, your dog might be doing their own version of interpretive dance in the background.

But wait, with the magic of "Stay," your dog transforms into a statue, holding their pose until you give the signal to move. It's the secret ingredient to capturing those adorable, memory-worthy moments without any photo-bombing from your furry friend.

Beyond photo-shoots, the "Stay" command is your go-to for various scenarios. From preventing your dog from dashing out the front door to keeping them safe during traffic or other hazards, "Stay" is the ultimate safety net. It's like saying, "Hold the fort, I'll be right back," and knowing your dog will dutifully obey.

How to introduce the command

Now, let's unveil the secret to teaching your dog the "Stay" command, turning them into a living statue of obedience. Here's how to get started:

1. Prepare Treats: Just like a movie star, your dog deserves treats as their reward. Gather small, tasty ones that your dog can't resist.
2. Choose a Quiet Space: Find a peaceful, distraction-free area to begin your training session.
3. Get Your Dog's Attention: Call your dog by their name with a cheerful, encouraging tone.
4. Start with 'Sit' or 'Down': It's easier to teach "Stay" from a sitting or lying-down position. Begin with your dog in one of these positions.
5. Show a Treat: Hold a treat in your hand, so your dog sees and smells it.
6. Use the Command: In a clear, firm voice, say "stay" while showing the treat.
7. Pause and Reward: Stand still for a few moments and then reward your dog with the treat and offer verbal praise like "Good stay!" or "Well done!"
8. Repeat: Practice this process multiple times in a single training session. Consistency is key.
9. Increase Duration: As your dog becomes more comfortable with "stay," gradually extend the time they must hold the position before

rewarding.

10. Use Hand Signals: You can incorporate a hand signal, like holding your palm out with your fingers extended, to reinforce the command.

11. Practice with Distractions: Gradually introduce controlled distractions during your training sessions to ensure your dog can stay focused.

12. Be Patient and Positive: Remember that patience and a positive attitude are essential during training. Every dog learns at their own pace.

13. Release Command: Teach a release command like "OK" or "Free" to signal to your dog when they can move again.

With regular practice, your dog will become a "Stay" superstar, ready to strike a pose or hold their ground when needed. It's all about safety, obedience, and creating those unforgettable moments with your faithful companion.

How the 'leave it' command prevented a potential emergency

While on a hike with my dog, Jack, he stumbled upon a tempting but dangerous snake. I panicked, but thankfully Jack had been trained rigorously with the "leave it" command. With adrenaline pumping, I shouted at him, and to my relief, he immediately backed away. This prevented a potential emergency, as the snake turned out to be venomous. The 'leave it' command, which we had practiced tirelessly, saved Jack from harm and me from a crisis. It reinforced the importance of dog training and quick thinking in unexpected situations, proving that a well-trained pet can truly be a lifesaver.

The 10-Minute Rule

The Concept of 10-Minute Training

Now, imagine you're about to embark on an epic training adventure with your four-legged friend. But wait, before you start envisioning a doggy version of a Rocky training montage, let's talk about the "10-Minute Rule."

The 10-Minute Rule is like the espresso shot of dog training – short, intense, and guaranteed to get tails wagging. It's all about keeping those training sessions brisk, clocking in at around 10 minutes each. Why? Well, let's face it, our furry companions have the attention span of a squirrel at a nut convention. So, instead of dragging out training for hours and risking both of you zoning out, we're going to condense it into power-packed, 10-minute bursts.

Now, here's the kicker – this rule is a lifesaver for those of us with busier schedules than a dog chasing its own tail. You can sneak these quick sessions in during your coffee breaks, while waiting for dinner to cook, or even when you're on hold during a work call (just make sure you mute the barking). It's dog training for the multitasker in you!

Now, onto the science bit – the neuroscience behind this approach is as cool as a cucumber (well, a cucumber to a human, maybe not to your dog). Short training sessions hit your pup's peak attention and focus. Picture this: every time they nail a command, their brain's like a fireworks show of dopamine – the feel-good neurotransmitter. It's the brain's way of saying, "Hey, that was awesome, let's do it again!"

So, with our 10-minute sessions, we're not just training dogs; we're hacking into their brains' reward system. We're the trainers, and dopamine is our secret weapon for creating lasting behavior changes. Pretty sneaky, right?

● Setting Up Your 10-Minute Sessions

Before you dive into these speedy training sessions, you'll need some gear – treats, a clicker, a leash, and toys. Think of them as your dog's training arsenal. The treats are like gold coins, the clicker is your dog's personal cheerleader, the leash is your trusty sidekick, and the toys are the grand prize at the end of it all.

Next, pick the perfect training battleground – a quiet, distraction-free space. Your backyard, a peaceful room, or even a fenced-in area all work wonders. We're talking "Zen garden" levels of tranquility here. No loud neighbors, no squirrel acrobatics, just you and your dog in training harmony.

Consistency is the name of the game. Instead of one marathon session, opt for multiple 10-minute sessions scattered throughout the day. Remember, dogs have shorter attention spans than a TikTok video, so short, frequent sessions are where the magic happens. Try timing these sessions with your dog's natural routine, like after meals or walks.

● Examples of 10-Minute Training Modules

Alright, it's showtime! Let's start with the basics: "Sit," "Stay," and "Come." Think of it as Dog Training 101 with a dash of Hollywood charm.

For "Sit," you'll hold a treat above your dog's head, and it's like they're auditioning for a canine talent show. They'll nail that sitting pose, and voila! Treat time! It's like winning an Oscar but with more tail wags.

Now, "Stay" is like teaching your dog the art of patience. You ask them to sit, take a step back like a mysterious magician, and return. If they stay seated, it's raining treats and praise – they've got the patience of a saint!

And finally, "Come" is your dog's cue to be the star of their own rom-com. Call their name, and when they make a grand entrance, shower them with treats and applause (well, at least the treats part).

Incorporating playtime into training

After mastering the basics, it's playtime! Think of it as the after-party of your training sessions. A quick game or a toy session is the way to go. You've worked hard, and now it's time for some fun. It's like rewarding yourself with a spa day after a week of tough workouts.

Advanced commands in 10-minute segments

Now, if your dog is feeling like a training superstar, you can move on to the advanced commands. "Lie Down," "Leave It," and "Heel" are the blockbuster sequels to your training journey. Be patient, use positive reinforcement like a Hollywood director with a megaphone, and keep those sessions short, sweet, and engaging. You'll have an obedient superstar on your hands in no time!

Remember, consistency and positive vibes are your allies in this training adventure. So, grab those treats, gear up, and let's turn your dog into a training sensation!

Now, let's dig deeper into why the 10-Minute Rule is the golden ticket to effective training, both for your pup and for you.

First off, it's a genius way to avoid cognitive overload in your dog. Think of it as avoiding the doggy equivalent of trying to binge-watch an entire season of a TV show in one sitting. Just like we humans can get mentally drained from marathon sessions, our furry friends can hit their mental limit too. By keeping training sessions short and snappy, we ensure they stay engaged and receptive.

Next up, short-term memory – or what we call the "in-one-ear-out-the-other" phenomenon. Dogs have a limited short-term memory span. So, if you throw too much at them in one go, it's like expecting them to remember a phone number without a pen and paper. Breaking training down into bite-sized sessions helps them retain and apply what they've learned effectively.

Lastly, it's all about optimizing that attention span. Most dogs have the focus of a toddler in a candy store, and that's just fine. The 10-Minute Rule taps into their natural capacity for concentration. Short sessions align with their ability to zone in on the task at hand, resulting in more productive training experiences. It's like teaching them to sprint instead of attempting a never-ending marathon.

● Advantages for the Trainer

Now, let's talk about you – the trainer-extraordinaire. Short, focused training sessions bring a truckload of benefits your way. First and foremost, they're the secret sauce for reducing fatigue and frustration.

Long sessions can be as draining as a never-ending game of fetch, and let's face it, that's not fun for anyone involved. Short, sweet sessions create a more enjoyable and effective training atmosphere.

Additionally, the 10-minute training rule is your time-saving superhero. In our whirlwind lives, finding an hour to train Fido can feel like trying to find a unicorn. But dedicating just 10 minutes? That's like fitting in a quick puppy power session during your daily routine. This regularity builds a routine that's crucial for effective learning and behavior modification.

But that's not all. Shorter sessions have another nifty trick up their sleeve – they supercharge your focus and preparation. Knowing you have a dedicated but brief training window encourages you to be well-prepared and organized. You come to the training party with a plan and a purpose. This level of preparation increases your chances of hitting those training goals and maintains a structured, goal-oriented approach.

Ultimately, the 10-minute rule is the magic wand that conjures up successful training outcomes and a better trainer-pet relationship. It turns the training process into a delightful and rewarding adventure for both you and your furry companion.

● Science-Backed Efficacy

Now, let's talk science. The 10-minute rule isn't just some arbitrary number pulled out of a hat; it's rooted in scientific research that's as solid as a bone your dog can't resist.

Studies in the fields of animal behavior and training have consistently shown that shorter, more frequent training sessions are the bee's knees when it comes to effective training. You see, dogs, much like us, aren't wired for hours of attention. Short sessions keep their focus and motivation levels high throughout the training journey.

This approach also gets a nod from behavioral psychology, particularly the fancy terms like "positive reinforcement" and "operant conditioning." Dogs are quick learners when they connect commands with immediate rewards. Short sessions ensure you can deliver those treats right on time, reinforcing those good behaviors and turbocharging the learning process.

But it's not just scientists in white lab coats who are fans of this rule. Veterinarians and canine experts everywhere give it a hearty thumbs up. Why? Because it keeps stress levels low for dogs, preventing physical and mental burnout during training. Plus, it's the antidote to boredom for both dogs and trainers, making the whole training experience enjoyable and effective.

In a nutshell, the 10-minute rule is science and practicality rolled into one, making it an invaluable tool for trainers looking to unlock the best results for their furry companions.

Commands to Start With

Let's bust a common myth, shall we? The belief that longer dog training sessions are always superior is as mythological as a three-headed hound guarding the gates of Hades. In the real world, shorter, focused sessions are often the key to unlocking the best results. Why? Because long training sessions can do a number on your pup's patience and attention span, leading to frustration and a "when will this end?" kind of vibe.

If you need proof, look no further than the world of Olympic dog agility competitions. These trainers are like the ninja warriors of the dog training world, conducting brief yet intense training with their canine comrades. The result? Remarkable agility and precision. These dogs shine because they're groomed for greatness through consistent short sessions, perfectly aligned with their "squirrel!" attention span.

Another aha moment comes from the world of police dog training. K-9 units, those heroes with four legs, train for high-stakes tasks like search and apprehension. How do they do it? Short, intense bursts of training. It's like a canine version of a SWAT team. This approach ensures they maintain a laser-like focus and top-notch precision during operations.

Now, let's address the "But my dog is special!" objection. We get it; your furball is one in a million. The 10-Minute Rule, suggesting 10 minutes of exercise per month of age, is a great starting point. But, like a fine-tailored suit, it can be adjusted to suit your dog's unique breed, age, and temperament.

For the furballs that resemble perpetual motion machines, like Border Collies, they might need a bit more exercise to keep them from rearranging the furniture when you're not looking. On the flip side, our squishy-faced pals like Bulldogs might need shorter, less intense sessions to avoid turning into canine pancakes.

Now, for our golden oldies, you can dial down the intensity a notch and keep a close eye on the fatigue meter. Young pups, on the other hand, can usually handle more vigorous play without breaking a sweat.

If your pup is a bit of a worrywart, shorter, more frequent sessions can be like a warm, reassuring hug to build their confidence.

Tips for slight adjustments without breaking the rule

1. Break up the routine. Instead of one marathon walk, opt for several short strolls to prevent them from considering you as a personal trainer.
2. Introduce brainy games like puzzle toys or obedience training to give their little noggins a workout.
3. Keep an eye out for signs of exhaustion, like dramatic panting, and adjust accordingly.
4. For the aquatically inclined, swimming or interactive water games can be gentle on the joints.
5. For the dogs with unique needs or health concerns, a chat with a professional is like a personalized training plan prescription.

Let's talk about what to do if your pup is more stubborn than a mule with a bone. First things first, dogs are like snowflakes; no two are the same. Some might need a bit more time to wrap their paws around those tricky commands.

Also, if your furball is a bit of a scatterbrain or an anxious bundle of nerves, it can slow down the progress train.

To supercharge your results without tossing the 10-Minute Rule out the window, try amping up the frequency of those short training sessions. Keep things engaging and rewarding with treats and positive vibes. Create a consistent environment with as few distractions as possible.

But, if you're still staring at that stubborn wagging tail without much progress, it might be time to call in the pros. This is especially true if your furball has decided that "I'll do what I want" is their life motto. A professional dog trainer or a canine behaviorist can swoop in like a training superhero, offering personalized guidance and a tailor-made training plan to conquer your unique challenges. Don't throw in the towel; remember, every dog is as unique as a fingerprint, and with a sprinkle of patience and the right guidance, most can be trained to be a top-notch companion.

The basics of dog training - where all the fun begins! Starting with the fundamentals is like laying the first brick in the doggy house of obedience. But why should we bother with the basics, you ask? Well, besides impressing your friends with your dog's impeccable manners, it's all about safety and sanity, for both you and your furry friend.

Imagine this: you're on a leisurely stroll in the park, and suddenly, your dog spots a squirrel on a mission. Without the basics like "stop" and "come," you're in for a wild ride, my friend. Mastering the basics is like giving your dog a universal remote control to navigate life's adventures. Commands like "sit," "stay," and "come" are your secret weapons to prevent your pup from turning your walk into a squirrel-chasing marathon.

But it's not just about avoiding parkour-style squirrel encounters. These basics build the foundation for a beautiful dog-owner friendship. Picture this: you're at the dog park, and your pup is making new furry pals. But when it's time to head home, a simple "come" command can save you from a game of hide-and-seek with your Houdini hound.

Now, let's talk about the benefits of mastering the basics, shall we?

Immediate obedience means you have a well-behaved co-pilot for life's journey. These basics are like your dog's GPS for good behavior, guiding them through everyday situations. And guess what? It gets even better!

Once your dog conquers the basics, they're ready to level up in the obedience game. It's like going from basic math to advanced calculus (well, maybe not that complicated, but you get the idea). With the basics firmly under their furry belt, learning advanced commands becomes a breeze. Positive reinforcement is your trusty sidekick in this training adventure, keeping your dog motivated and tail-waggingly happy.

Now, let's dive into the science behind starting simple, shall we? Dogs, like humans, have a learning curve that varies with age. Puppies are like sponges, soaking up knowledge faster than a thirsty camel in the desert. Adolescents might be a bit scatterbrained, but they're up for a challenge. Adults are steady learners, while seniors might need a bit more patience.

Starting with the basics aligns perfectly with your dog's brainpower at different stages of life. It's like giving them the right puzzle pieces for their cognitive development. Simple commands, like "sit" and "stay," are like the beginner's level in a video game - they boost your dog's confidence and set the stage for tackling more complex tasks.

So, there you have it, the science-backed wisdom of starting with the basics. It's not just about teaching your dog manners; it's about building a strong foundation for a lifelong partnership. Plus, who doesn't want a dog that can impress with tricks beyond just rolling over and playing dead? So, grab those treats, put on your training hat, and get ready for a journey of canine enlightenment!

Basic commands serve as the foundation for any training program because they establish communication between a pet and its owner. Commands like "sit," "stay," and "come" lay the groundwork for obedience, safety, and socialization. They help dogs understand boundaries and expectations, creating a positive and structured learning environment.

In everyday life, these basic commands are essential for safety, ensuring that dogs don't run into danger or create chaos in public spaces. Advanced training builds upon these basics, teaching more complex tasks like agility or service dog work. These commands enable dogs to develop discipline, problem-solving skills, and the ability to assist people with disabilities or excel in various dog sports, enhancing their role as loyal companions and versatile partners.

Now, let's talk prerequisites for teaching these fundamental commands. Timing, rewards, and consistency are crucial in dog training. Timing involves giving commands precisely when the desired behavior occurs, reinforcing the connection between action and command. Rewards, like treats or praise, motivate the dog to repeat the behavior. Consistency is key; everyone in the household should use the same commands and reward system.

Gauge your dog's readiness by assessing their attention span and responsiveness. Start with simple commands like "sit" and "stay" in a distraction-free environment. If your dog readily obeys, gradually introduce more commands. Monitor their body language; a wagging tail and eager demeanor suggest readiness. Be patient, as each dog learns at its own pace. Adjust the complexity of commands as your dog becomes more proficient.

Now, let's discuss setting up your training sessions for success. To effectively train a dog in basic commands, choosing the right environment is crucial. Opt for a quiet, distraction-free area initially, gradually progressing to more challenging settings.

Clickers, treats, and leashes are valuable tools in this process. The clicker serves as a precise marker for desired behavior, while treats act as positive reinforcement. Leashes aid in control and safety. Start with simple commands like sit, stay, and come, using the clicker and treats as rewards when the dog complies. With the right foundation and approach, you'll have your furry friend mastering these basic commands in no time!

The role of vocal cues and body language

The role of vocal cues and body language is essential in effective dog training. Dogs are highly attuned to human communication, both verbal and non-verbal. Here, we'll delve into the significance of these cues and how to use them effectively to communicate with your furry companion.

Vocal cues: Dogs can learn to associate specific words or phrases with actions or behaviors. For instance, using "sit" as a cue for your dog to sit down or "stay" to command them to remain in place. Consistency in your vocal cues is key. Use the same words or phrases each time you want your dog to perform a particular action. Over time, they will learn to recognize and respond to these vocal cues.

However, it's not just the words you say; it's how you say them. Dogs can pick up on your tone and intonation. A cheerful, upbeat tone is more likely to motivate and engage your dog, while a stern tone may signal that they've done something wrong. Keep your vocal cues clear, positive, and consistent to enhance your dog's understanding and responsiveness.

Body language: Dogs are experts at reading human body language. Your posture, gestures, and facial expressions convey important information to your furry friend. For example, standing tall and extending your hand with an open palm can signal a greeting or a command like "shake." Conversely, leaning forward with a pointed finger may indicate a directive like "come."

It's crucial to be aware of your body language during training. Your dog will respond not only to what you say but also to how you physically express yourself. Maintain an open and relaxed posture to create a welcoming and comfortable training environment. Avoid looming over your dog, as this can be perceived as threatening. By aligning your body language with your vocal cues, you'll enhance the clarity and effectiveness of your communication.

In the following chapters, we'll explore specific vocal cues and body language techniques tailored to various tricks and commands. Mastering these communication tools will help you and your dog achieve success in your training journey.

As we've seen, vocal cues and body language play a crucial role in dog training, helping to convey our expectations and establish effective communication with our furry companions. But let me take you on a walk through a picturesque park where a heartwarming sight awaits, highlighting the practical application of these cues.

One sunny afternoon, you're enjoying a leisurely walk in a picturesque park, where families and their four-legged companions gather to soak up the beauty of nature. As you stroll along a tree-lined path, you notice a heartwarming sight: a family with their exuberant Golden Retriever, Bella.

Bella is a beautiful, spirited dog with a heart full of curiosity. She's exploring the wonders of the park, her tail wagging enthusiastically as she sniffs flowers, chases butterflies, and greets fellow dogs with boundless energy. The family is equally joyous, relishing the opportunity to spend quality time in the great outdoors.

As you continue your walk, you overhear the father, John, instructing Bella. "Bella, stay!" he commands firmly. You glance over and see Bella, with ears perked and eyes fixed on her owner, remaining perfectly still. Her body quivers with anticipation, but she obeys the "Stay" command faithfully.

John's daughter, Emily, has a mischievous glint in her eye as she holds a Frisbee in her hand. She takes a few steps back, ready to launch it across the park for Bella to chase. However, before she releases the Frisbee, John utters another command, "Come, Bella!" he calls out, his voice filled with affection.

Bella's reaction is nothing short of remarkable. She immediately abandons her playful stance, leaves the Frisbee untouched, and races back to John with unwavering obedience. In a split second, she's by his side, waiting for further instructions.

As you watch this unfold, you can't help but be impressed by the family's diligent training and Bella's responsiveness. The "Stay" and "Come" commands have not only demonstrated Bella's discipline but have also potentially saved her from a dangerous situation.

At that very moment, you notice a bicyclist whizzing past the park's entrance, speeding along the path. If Bella hadn't obeyed the "Stay" and "Come" commands, she might have dashed across the path in pursuit of the Frisbee, putting herself at risk of colliding with the fast-moving cyclist.

The family's well-trained dog is safe, happy, and blissfully unaware of the potential danger that the "Stay" and "Come" commands have helped her avoid. You can't help but smile, appreciating the power of training and the importance of these fundamental commands in ensuring a dog's safety and well-being.

"You've aced the doggy ABCs, now let's kick it up a notch and dive into the doggy PhD's! Get ready for Chapter 3: Advancing to the Next Level - Advanced Commands."

3

Advancing to the Next Level: Advanced Commands

"Mastering basic commands lays the groundwork, but it's the advanced training that truly unlocks your dog's full potential."
— Cesar Millan, Renowned Dog Trainer and Behaviorist

* * *

Some breeds, like Border Collies, Poodles, and German Shepherds, can understand and respond to over 1,000 different words and commands. This astounding linguistic comprehension highlights the remarkable cognitive abilities of dogs and their capacity for learning and communication, rivaling the language skills of some young children.

Why Advance Commands are more than Just Tricks?

Now that you've conquered the canine ABCs, it's time to unlock the secret world of doggy genius! Welcome to Chapter 3: Advancing to the Next Level - Advanced Commands, where we'll delve into the art of unleashing your pup's inner Einstein.

Advanced commands aren't just about showing off your dog's brain-power (though that's a fun bonus). They're a vital key to a happy and fulfilled pup. Think of it as enrolling your furry friend in a prestigious canine university, where they major in mental stimulation.

So, why should you bother with advanced commands, you ask? Well, here's the scoop: it's all about keeping your dog's noggin engaged. Just like us, dogs can get bored, and that boredom can lead to all sorts of shenanigans, from redecorating your living room with chewed-up pillows to serenading the neighborhood with endless barking.

But fear not, because advanced training is here to save the day! By challenging your dog's mind with activities like puzzle toys, obedience training, and interactive games, you're providing them with mental gymnastics that keep their brain cells firing. This isn't just about preventing boredom; it's about creating a happier, smarter, and better-behaved furry companion.

Imagine your dog, let's call her Luna, used to be a restless whirlwind of energy, causing chaos left and right. She'd chew on furniture, dig up the garden, and turn every pillow into a fluffy battleground. But then, Luna embarked on her advanced training journey, and oh, what a transformation! As she tackled intricate commands and faced mental challenges head-on, a wave of calmness washed over her.

Luna's anxiety and restlessness began to fade, replaced by a newfound sense of purpose and fulfillment. It was like she'd discovered the meaning of life (or at least the meaning of "roll over" and "fetch"). Her journey from chaos to contentment is a testament to the magic of advanced training.

But it's not all about preventing destruction and promoting zen-like calmness. Advanced commands also serve some pretty nifty real-life purposes. Imagine your dog being your trusty sidekick, ready to spring into action in emergency situations. Commands like "retrieve," "find," and "call for help" can be total game-changers.

Need your medication? No problem, your dog can fetch it. Can't find your phone? Your canine detective will track it down. Worried about intruders? Your furry alarm system is on the case. These commands aren't just impressive party tricks; they're potentially lifesaving skills.

And hey, advanced training isn't just about emergencies. It's about making your daily routines smoother and more efficient. Commands like "fetch," "stay," and "leave it" can turn your dog into the ultimate helper. They can retrieve items, stay out of your way when you're busy, and prevent them from munching on things they shouldn't.

But here's the icing on the training cake: advanced commands aren't just about making your dog smarter and more helpful. They're also about strengthening your bond. When you and your dog tackle complex tasks together, it's like embarking on an epic adventure.

You'll communicate, cooperate, and celebrate your successes as a team. Your dog's progress becomes a source of pride and joy, reinforcing the trust between you. This bond extends beyond training, creating a profound connection based on teamwork and shared achievements.

But it's not just about your dog's growth; it's about yours too. As you witness your pup mastering complex commands, you'll feel a sense of accomplishment and pride. The shared journey strengthens your relationship, builds trust, and improves communication. Plus, it offers a comforting sense of security, knowing that your dog is not just a companion but a reliable partner.

Let me introduce you to Bella and Max. They embarked on an advanced training adventure that transformed them into a remarkable team. Max's "fetch" command became a real-life hero as he saved Bella's phone from a perilous cliff's edge during a hike. But beyond obedience, their training strengthened their bond, turning them into an unstoppable duo.

Through this journey, Bella and Max discovered the true meaning of partnership, loyalty, and the incredible power of investing in their shared growth. So, get ready to embark on your own journey of canine enlightenment as we explore the world of advanced commands in Chapter 3!

Advanced commands involve mental stimulation. This is crucial for a happy dog. Challenging their mind through activities like puzzle toys, obedience training, and interactive games offers numerous benefits. It helps prevent boredom, reduces destructive behavior, and enhances their problem-solving skills. This mental engagement also strengthens the owner-dog bond and contributes to a content and well-balanced canine companion.

Engaging their minds through activities, puzzles, and training not only prevents boredom but also promotes cognitive development. This mental exercise can reduce anxiety and destructive behaviors, leading to a content and well-balanced canine companion.

Advanced training provides crucial mental stimulation for dogs, ensuring their happiness and well-being. In a compelling case study, a dog named Luna experienced a transformative journey. Initially restless and prone to destructive behavior, Luna's transition to contentment became evident as she engaged in advanced training.

Through the challenges of learning intricate commands, Luna's mind was stimulated, reducing anxiety and restlessness. She found a sense of purpose and fulfillment in mastering complex tasks, ultimately leading to a more balanced and contented life. This case study exemplifies the profound impact that advanced training can have on a dog's mental and emotional well-being, underlining the importance of mental stimulation in keeping our canine companions happy and fulfilled.

●**Practical Uses for Advanced Commands**

Advanced commands in dog training go beyond the basics and have practical uses, particularly in emergency situations. Commands such as "retrieve," "find," and "call for help" can be invaluable in times of need. For instance, a dog trained to retrieve essential items like medication or a phone can aid individuals with mobility issues or medical emergencies. Dogs that can locate a missing person or alert to hazards like fires or intruders contribute to enhanced safety. These advanced commands can be lifesaving, making them crucial components of comprehensive dog training for both everyday life and unforeseen emergencies.

These commands enhance daily routines by simplifying tasks and improving efficiency. For example, commands like "fetch" can help retrieve items, while "stay" keeps the dog out of the way during chores. "Leave it" prevents them from interfering with potentially harmful objects. "Close the door" and "turn off the lights" are examples of advanced commands that contribute to a smoother daily life. These commands minimize interruptions and enable dogs to actively participate in household tasks, making routines more streamlined.

In real-life dog training scenarios, advanced commands shine through their practicality. Dogs trained to "search and rescue" locate missing persons, aiding in life-saving missions. "Medical alert" dogs sense health issues and alert their owners, providing crucial support. "Assistance dogs" can perform tasks like opening doors or fetching items for individuals with disabilities, enhancing their independence. These examples showcase how advanced commands empower dogs to be invaluable companions and lifesavers in various real-world situations.

When undertaken together by an owner and their canine companion, is a powerful trust-building experience. It demands communication, patience, and collaboration. As the dog masters complex commands, the owner witnesses their pet's progress, reinforcing their bond. Mutual understanding and cooperation create a strong sense of trust and reliability between them. This trust extends beyond training, enhancing the overall relationship and creating a deep emotional connection based on teamwork and shared achievement.

The process of training and witnessing a pet master complex commands also fosters a deep sense of accomplishment, enhancing the owner's self-esteem and pride. This shared achievement strengthens the bond, fostering trust and improving communication, leading to a more fulfilling and harmonious relationship. It also provides a sense of security, knowing that their dog can assist in emergencies. In essence, advanced training not only enriches a dog's life but also brings joy, confidence, and peace of mind to the owner.

Once, Bella and her dog, Max, embarked on advanced training. They faced challenges, but their efforts paid off. Max's newfound skills not only impressed onlookers but also drew them closer. The training sessions became moments of connection, trust, and shared achievement.

One day, while hiking, Max's "fetch" command saved Bella's phone from a cliff's edge. Their bond had become unbreakable. Beyond obedience, advanced training strengthened their relationship, turning them into a remarkable team. Through this journey, Bella and Max discovered the true meaning of partnership, loyalty, and the incredible power of investing in their shared growth.

When your dog is ready for advanced training, it's like they've graduated from the basic obedience school and are now entering the realm of higher education. You'll notice a combination of behaviors and skills that indicate their readiness. These signs include:

1. **Consistent Obedience**: Your dog reliably follows basic commands such as sit, stay, and come, both at home and in different environments. It's like they've become the Einstein of obedience.
2. **Strong Focus**: Your dog can maintain attention on you, even when there are distractions present. This focus is crucial for advanced training and is like having a dog with laser-focused determination.
3. **Excellent Recall**: Your dog comes when called, even when off-leash, demonstrating a high level of trust and responsiveness. It's as if they've mastered the art of teleportation, but in a canine way.

4. **Calm Demeanor**: Your dog exhibits good behavior and can control its excitement, which is essential for more advanced and complex training tasks. It's like they've taken a chill pill for dogs.

5. **Eagerness to Learn**: Your dog shows enthusiasm for training sessions, quickly grasping new commands, and displaying a willingness to work and learn. They're basically the canine version of a bookworm, eager to soak up knowledge.

6. **Solid Foundation**: Your dog has a strong foundation in basic training skills, making it easier to build upon with more advanced commands and tasks. Think of it as having a sturdy base for a towering doggy skyscraper.

7. **Social Skills**: Your dog interacts well with other dogs and people, indicating that they can handle the social aspects of advanced training, such as group classes or competitions. They're basically the social butterflies of the dog world.

These signs collectively show that your dog is ready to move on to advanced training, which may include agility, specialized skills, or more advanced obedience commands.

However, before moving on to advanced commands, your dog should have a solid understanding of basic commands. These basic commands typically include:

1. **Sit**: Your dog should sit when asked and remain in that position until given another command. It's like having a furry, four-legged statue on command.

2. **Stay**: Your dog should be able to stay in place until you release them. It's like having a pause button for your pup.

3. **Come**: Your dog should reliably come when called, even in

distracting environments. It's like having a canine boomerang.

4. **Down**: Your dog should lie down on command. It's like having a built-in doggy "relax" mode.

5. **Leave It**: Your dog should understand not to pick up or interact with something when told to "leave it." It's like having a mini K-9 detective who knows what to avoid.

6. **Heel**: Your dog should walk calmly beside you on a loose leash without pulling. It's like having a perfectly synchronized doggy dance partner.

7. **Off**: Your dog should know to get off furniture or not jump on people when you say "off." It's like having a well-mannered, non-jumping furry friend.

8. **No**: Your dog should understand a general "no" command to stop an undesirable behavior. It's like having a canine referee to call fouls.

9. **Wait**: Your dog should pause or wait before moving forward, such as before crossing a street. It's like having a built-in "red light, green light" system.

Once your dog has a strong grasp of these basic commands and responds consistently, you can consider moving on to more advanced training. Advanced commands can include tricks, advanced obedience commands, agility, scent work, or specialized tasks, depending on your goals and your dog's abilities. Building a strong foundation with basic commands is essential for successful advanced training.

Setting up for success in advanced dog training methods requires careful planning and preparation. First, choosing the right environment is crucial. Ensure it's quiet, free from distractions and safe for both you and your dog. A controlled space makes it easier to focus on training.

Gather the necessary training tools. For advanced training, you might need items like clickers, target sticks, agility equipment, and specialized collars or harnesses. Choose tools that align with your training goals and your dog's needs.

Once you have what you need, create a training schedule. Consistency is key in advanced training. Plan regular sessions, keeping them short and engaging. Incorporate a variety of exercises to prevent boredom and maintain your dog's interest. Track your progress and adjust the schedule as needed based on your dog's responsiveness.

Also, when pursuing advanced dog training, set realistic goals. Understand that complex behaviors take time. Focus on specific objectives like advanced obedience commands or agility skills. Be patient and avoid expecting instant results.

Slow progress is common in advanced training. Stay calm and avoid frustration. Analyze what's causing the delay—perhaps distractions or insufficient motivation. Adjust your expectations, break tasks into smaller steps, and celebrate small victories. Consistency and repetition are key.

To adapt training tactics, assess your dog's response. If a method isn't working, try alternatives. Use positive reinforcement, treats, or toys to motivate. Seek professional guidance if needed. Maintain a flexible approach, as each dog is unique. Modify your techniques based on your dog's behavior and preferences. Remember, advanced training is a journey that requires adaptability and persistence to achieve your desired outcomes. And, most importantly, keep a sense of humor along the way because sometimes your dog might just outsmart you with their clever canine antics!

Roadblocks and How to Overcome Them

Navigating the road to advanced dog training can sometimes feel like taking a cross-country road trip with a few unexpected detours. But fear not, because we've got a road map for overcoming common roadblocks in advanced dog training:

1. **Lack of Solid Foundation**: If your dog's basic training is as shaky as a house of cards in a windstorm, it can hinder advanced training. The solution? Go back to basics, reinforcing those fundamental commands before diving into the advanced stuff. It's like fixing the foundation of your doggy house before adding a second story.

2. **Distractions**: Dogs are pros at getting distracted, especially when there are squirrels involved. To overcome this, start with minimal distractions and gradually level up. It's like teaching your dog to focus amidst a squirrel convention.

3. **Inconsistency**: When everyone in the family has a different set of rules, your dog can end up as confused as a cat at a dog show. Establish clear and consistent training guidelines within your household. Think of it as having a unified doggy constitution.

4. **Physical Limitations**: Sometimes, health issues or physical limitations can throw a wrench into your dog's training gears. Consult with a veterinarian to address these concerns and modify exercises accordingly. It's like adjusting your workout routine after a visit to the doctor.

5. **Boredom**: Just like humans, dogs can get bored with the same old routine. Keep training sessions fresh by introducing new challenges, tricks, or variations. It's like spicing up your dog's training menu.

6. **Over-training**: Dogs can suffer from training fatigue, just like we can after a long day of work. Keep sessions short and focused,

breaking complex tasks into manageable steps. It's like offering your dog a training appetizer instead of a full-course meal.

7. **Fear or Anxiety**: Dogs with fears and anxieties may need a little extra TLC during training. Gradual exposure to their fears in a positive manner and desensitization techniques can help. Think of it as helping your dog conquer their fears one training session at a time.

8. **Complex Commands**: Some advanced commands can be as confusing as a Rubik's Cube for your pup. Break these commands into smaller, digestible steps, and reward their incremental progress. It's like solving a puzzle one piece at a time.

9. **Handler Frustration**: Your own frustration can throw a monkey wrench into the training gears. Stay patient, positive, and calm during sessions, and don't be afraid to take a breather if needed. Think of it as practicing your own "zen" during training.

10. **Training Method Incompatibility**: Not all dogs respond to the same training methods. Be flexible and experiment with different techniques to find what works best for your dog. It's like trying out different recipes until you find your dog's favorite training treat.

11. **Lack of Motivation**: Some dogs lose interest in treats faster than a kid loses interest in spinach. Use a variety of rewards, including playtime, praise, and different treats, to keep their motivation high. Think of it as keeping a well-stocked treat arsenal.

12. **Plateau in Learning**: Dogs, just like us, can hit a learning plateau. Change up your routines, introduce new challenges, and keep their minds engaged to push through it. It's like overcoming writer's block during a training session.

Overcoming these roadblocks requires adaptability, patience, and a deep understanding of your dog's unique needs and limitations. Seeking guidance from a professional dog trainer can be like having a GPS to navigate these training obstacles. An expert can provide valuable guidance and ensure the safety and effectiveness of the training process.

When seeking out such services, several key factors should be considered. First, qualifications and certifications from reputable organizations like the Association of Professional Dog Trainers (APDT) can indicate expertise. Their experience working with dogs of similar breed and behavior issues is crucial. Look for trainers who use positive reinforcement methods, as they are generally more effective and humane. Furthermore, the trainer should have good communication skills to teach both the dog and owner effectively.

Financial considerations vary based on location, but investing in professional training for complex issues can save money in the long run by preventing costly problems and ensuring a happy, well-behaved pet. However, owners should weigh the costs against their budget and the severity of the dog's issues, opting for the best value for their specific situation.

Celebrating Small Wins

Now, let's talk about the fun part – celebrating those small wins! In advanced dog training, it's like throwing a party every time your dog conquers a new skill. Positive reinforcement is the name of the game, and dogs absolutely thrive on it.

The types of rewards that work best include food treats, toys, and verbal praise. These rewards should be tailored to the dog's preferences. It's like knowing your dog's favorite snacks and keeping them on hand for those special moments.

But celebrating achievements isn't just about the treats; it has a profound psychological impact on your furry friend. Dogs, just like humans, thrive on positive feedback. Recognizing those small wins boosts their self-esteem, confidence, and motivation to keep learning. It's like giving them a standing ovation after a flawless performance.

So, in advanced training, don't forget to throw a mini celebration for your dog's victories. It not only makes them feel like the training superstar they are but also fosters a deeper bond between you and your four-legged partner in crime. And who doesn't love a reason to celebrate with their best furry friend?

The Psychological Science behind Rewards

Let's dive into the fascinating world of the psychological science behind rewards in dog training. It's like uncovering the secret sauce that makes your dog willingly follow commands.

Positive Reinforcement Unveiled

Positive reinforcement in canine training is all about rewarding your dog with something it finds utterly pleasurable immediately after displaying a desired behavior. Think of it as giving your pup a standing ovation for a stellar performance. For instance, when your dog sits on command and you shower them with treats or praise, that's positive reinforcement in action. It's the art of encouraging good behavior rather than punishing the unwanted ones.

Now, here's where it gets interesting. Positive reinforcement takes a different route compared to its stern cousin, negative reinforcement.

In positive reinforcement, you're adding a reward to encourage the behavior you want. Meanwhile, negative reinforcement involves removing an aversive stimulus to achieve the same goal. For example, when you release tension on the leash as your dog stops pulling, that's negative reinforcement. Positive reinforcement is all about rewarding the behaviors you desire, while negative reinforcement focuses on eliminating the ones you don't.

The Science is In: Positive Reinforcement Rocks

Scientific research consistently gives a thumbs-up to positive reinforcement as an effective and humane training method. Studies have shown that it leads to more desirable and lasting results in dogs, all without causing fear or stress. It's like teaching your dog with kindness and encouragement instead of sternness. This approach aligns beautifully with the principles of operant conditioning, creating a positive and cooperative learning experience for dogs. Plus, it strengthens the bond between dogs and their owners, making it a win-win for everyone involved.

Types of Rewards: Treats, Toys, and Love

When it comes to rewards, it's like having a treasure chest of goodies for your dog. Let's explore the loot:

- **Food Rewards**: These are like the golden tickets of dog training. Highly effective and immediately appealing to your furry friend. They come with the perk of precise timing, making them great for shaping behaviors. However, be mindful of portion control to avoid unwanted weight gain. Also, keep the treats varied to prevent picky eaters from getting bored.

- **Toys**: Picture this – your dog's face lighting up with joy as they see their favorite toy. Toys can be excellent motivators, especially for those energetic breeds who can't resist a game of fetch. They're like the playmates that add an element of fun and exercise to training sessions. However, not all dogs are equally excited about toys, so choose ones that align with your dog's preferences.
- **Verbal Praise and Petting**: These rewards are like warm hugs and encouraging words. They provide important emotional rewards, strengthening the bond between you and your dog. It's like telling them, "You're doing great, buddy!" Use these rewards alongside others to reinforce desired behaviors. Keep in mind that dogs have different sensitivities to praise, and while some lap it up like ice cream, others may prefer tangible rewards.

Timing is Everything

In the world of dog training, timing is the secret sauce. Imagine it as capturing a perfect moment on camera. The immediacy of delivering rewards is crucial. Dogs have the attention span of a squirrel, so they link rewards most strongly with the behavior when given immediately. Delayed rewards can lead to confusion, making it harder for your dog to understand which action earned the reward. It's like showing your dog a treat and then making them wait an hour – they'll wonder what they did to deserve it!

The Art of 'Marking' the Behavior

Now, here's where precision comes into play. The concept of 'marking' the behavior involves using a marker, like a clicker or a specific word, to precisely signal the desired action the moment it occurs. It's like telling your dog, "Bingo! That's exactly what I wanted!" This marker acts as a bridge, connecting the behavior with the forthcoming reward. It helps your dog understand what they're being rewarded for, like a spotlight on the stage of their performance.

In a case study comparing correct and incorrect timing, correct timing leads to a dog associating the reward with the exact behavior you desire, reinforcing it effectively. It's like giving them a gold star right when they've aced the test. Incorrect timing, on the other hand, can confuse your dog, making it unclear which action led to the reward, potentially hindering the training progress. In summary, timing and immediacy in reward delivery are fundamental elements for successful dog training, like the key to unlocking your dog's potential.

Transitioning from Basic to Advanced with Rewards

Let's embark on the journey of transitioning from basic to advanced commands with the magic of rewards. It's like leveling up in a video game, but the rewards are your dog's newfound skills.

Timing is Everything: Mastering the Basics

You've been diligently teaching your dog the basics like sit, stay, and come, and now it's time to take things up a notch. This usually happens around 6-8 months of age when your dog has become a seasoned pro at the fundamental commands. But remember, patience is the key; your dog should consistently respond to these existing commands before you start introducing new ones.

As you embark on this exciting journey, keep a balance. Continue practicing the basics, but gradually decrease their frequency in your training sessions. We don't want your dog to forget them, after all. Instead of repeatedly asking your dog to sit, for example, focus on introducing those advanced commands.

Motivation with Rewards: The Treats and Toys Strategy

To keep your dog motivated and engaged, make treats or toys your trusty sidekicks. Short and positive training sessions work wonders, and remember to be patient throughout the process. Clear and consistent cues are your secret weapon, and when your dog nails it, don't forget to reinforce their correct responses with rewards.

Command Combos: Building Complexity

Think of your dog's training like a series of dance moves. Start with the basic steps and then combine them to create a masterpiece. Ask your dog to sit and then stay before offering the reward. This helps your dog understand that they must follow a sequence of instructions to earn a well-deserved reward.

Reward your dog for successfully executing a sequence of commands, and gradually reduce the frequency of rewards while still providing occasional ones to reinforce the behavior. It's like giving your dog a gold star for acing the choreography.

Distracting Situations: The Real-Life Test

Life is full of distractions, and your dog needs to be ready for them. Training with distractions is like preparing for the big stage. Start with mild distractions, such as low-level noise, and reward your dog for maintaining focus on your commands. Slowly increase the difficulty by exposing your dog to more distracting environments.

In the midst of distractions, rewards become even more critical. Think of them as the spotlight that keeps your dog's attention on you. If your dog stays calm around a new person or another animal, reward them with treats, playtime, or affection. This reinforces the idea that listening to you is more rewarding than being distracted by the world.

Steering Clear of Pitfalls: Common Mistakes and How to Avoid Them

Now, let's avoid some common pitfalls in this training adventure:

- **Over-Rewarding**: Don't go overboard with treats; it can lead to a portly pup and loss of interest. Opt for healthier, low-calorie treats, and mix in non-food rewards like praise or play. Strike that perfect balance to maintain your dog's motivation.
- **Inconsistent Rewards**: Keep things consistent to avoid confusion. Your dog might wonder why they're only getting treats sometimes. Stick to a consistent reward schedule for better results, and use verbal cues or hand signals consistently.
- **Phasing Out Rewards**: As your dog becomes a pro, start reducing treat frequency. Gradually replace treats with other rewards, like affection or toys, and let your dog find intrinsic enjoyment in the desired behavior. Transition from training environments to real-world situations, where good behavior is rewarded with real-life perks like walks or playtime.

By navigating these training waters with precision, you'll unlock your dog's potential and create a bond that's stronger than ever. It's a journey filled with achievements, like discovering the hidden talents of your four-legged companion.

Start introducing new commands when your dog has mastered the basics like sit, stay, and come. This usually happens around 6-8 months of age. Be sure your dog consistently responds to existing commands before adding new ones.

Fine-Tuning the Transition: Balancing Basics and Advanced Training

As you continue on this thrilling journey of transitioning your dog from basic to advanced commands, it's important to master the art of balance. Your dog has conquered the basics like a pro - sit, stay, and come are second nature to them by now, usually around the age of 6-8 months. Before diving headfirst into advanced commands, make sure your furry friend consistently responds to the existing commands. It's like ensuring your foundation is rock-solid before building the skyscraper of advanced training.

While introducing these new, exciting commands, don't forget about the basics. Keep them in your training repertoire, but gradually decrease their frequency in your sessions. We want to prevent your dog from forgetting those essential skills. For instance, instead of repeatedly asking your dog to sit within a single training session, shift your focus towards the advanced commands that await.

Motivation: The Treats and Toys Strategy, Continued

Treats and toys remain your trusty allies on this journey. They're like the sparks of motivation that keep your dog's training engine running. Keep your training sessions short, sweet, and positive. Patience is your guiding star, and those clear and consistent cues are your compass. When your dog gets it right, don't forget to reinforce their correct responses with well-deserved rewards.

The Symphony of Commands: Building Complexity

Now, let's talk about creating symphonies of commands. Just like composing a beautiful piece of music, you can combine commands to build complexity. Imagine asking your dog to sit and then stay before unveiling the grand finale – the reward. This orchestration of commands teaches your dog that they must follow a harmonious sequence of instructions to earn their well-earned ovation.

But that's not all. It's time to celebrate the crescendo. Reward your dog for successfully executing a sequence of commands. Gradually, as your dog becomes a virtuoso, reduce the frequency of rewards, but still sprinkle in occasional ones to reinforce their virtuosity.

To paint you a clearer picture, let's take "sit," "stay," and "come" as an example. You start with "sit," then gracefully progress to "stay" while taking a few steps back, and finally, like the grand finale of a fireworks show, you use "come" to call your dog back to you. Each step is a note in this musical masterpiece, and every note deserves applause – or in this case, a reward.

The Real-World Challenge: Training with Distractions

Life isn't always a quiet concert hall; sometimes it's a bustling city street. To prepare your dog for the real-world challenge, you need to train a midst distractions. Start with mild distractions, like a soft background noise, and reward your dog for maintaining focus on your commands. Gradually turn up the volume by exposing your dog to more distracting environments.

In the presence of these distractions, rewards become the spotlight that keeps your dog's attention on you. Imagine your dog staying calm around a new person or another animal; that's their moment to shine. Reward them with treats, playtime, or affection. This reinforces the idea that listening to you is like winning the biggest prize.

Navigating the Training Waters: Common Mistakes and How to Stay Afloat

Now, let's steer clear of some common pitfalls on this training voyage:

- **Over-Rewarding**: Avoid the temptation to shower your dog with treats during training; it can lead to a portly pup and a loss of interest. Opt for healthier, low-calorie treats and mix in non-food rewards like praise or play. Finding the right balance keeps your dog's motivation soaring. Monitor your dog's response, and adjust the reward frequency accordingly.
- **Inconsistent Rewards**: Consistency is key to avoid confusion. Your dog might wonder why they're only getting treats sometimes. Stick to a consistent reward schedule for smoother sailing, and use those verbal cues or hand signals consistently.
- **Phasing Out Rewards**: As your dog's skills blossom, start decreasing treat frequency. Gradually replace treats with other rewards and use treats only intermittently. Encourage your dog to find joy in the desired behavior itself, like letting them explore and play in a controlled environment. Transition from the training grounds to

real-life situations, where good behavior is rewarded with real-life treasures like walks or playtime.

By skillfully navigating these training waters, you'll unlock your dog's full potential, and your bond will become stronger than ever. It's a journey filled with milestones and delightful surprises, like discovering the true depth of your four-legged companion's abilities.

Advanced Commands

The "Heel" Command

"Heel" is considered advanced because it requires precision, focus, and consistent execution. It goes beyond basic commands like "Sit" and "Stay" because it involves your dog's ability to maintain a specific position while in motion. Achieving this level of discipline and control takes time and patience.

The "Heel" command also has significant safety benefits. It reduces the risk of your dog lunging at other animals, people, or vehicles, which can lead to accidents or aggressive behavior. It also minimizes the chances of your dog escaping from its leash, keeping it safe and secure during walks.

It is invaluable in various real-world situations. For example, when crossing a busy street, your dog heeling by your side ensures that it won't dart into traffic. In crowded places like parks, it prevents your dog from jumping on strangers or other dogs. Additionally, it enhances the overall walking experience, making it more enjoyable for both you and your pet.

●Step-by-Step Training for 'Heel'

Training your dog to "heel" is an important command for leash walking. Here's a step-by-step guide:

1. **Preparation:** Gather high-value treats or rewards and have your dog on a leash and collar or harness.Find a quiet, low-distraction environment for training.
2. **Start Walking:** Begin walking with your dog on your preferred side (usually the left) with a loose leash. Keep your dog's attention with treats in your pocket or treat pouch.
3. **Use the Command:** When you want your dog to heel, say "heel" in a firm but friendly tone.
4. **Encourage Position:** Guide your dog to the desired heel position, which is typically with their shoulder in line with your leg. Use your hand with the treat to lure them into this position.
5. **Reward Heeling:** As soon as your dog is in the correct heel position, immediately reward them with a treat and offer praise. Keep the leash loose during this process.
6. **Maintain Focus:** Keep your dog's attention by holding more treats in your hand, occasionally giving rewards for staying in the heel position.
7. **Short Training Sessions:** Keep training sessions short and positive. 10-15 minutes at a time is usually sufficient.
8. **Practice and Consistency:** Practice heeling in different locations and gradually add more distractions as your dog improves.
9. **Gradual Phasing Out of Treats:** As your dog becomes proficient, reduce the frequency of treat rewards but continue to praise them

for heeling correctly.

10. **Release Command:** Introduce a "release" command like "okay" to let your dog know they are no longer required to heel. Use this to signal the end of the heeling exercise.

11. **Use Positive Reinforcement:** Consistently use positive reinforcement (treats, praise, and occasional play) to encourage your dog to maintain the heel position.

12. **Consistency is Key:** Be consistent with your commands, rewards, and expectations to reinforce proper heeling behavior.

Remember that patience and consistency are crucial in teaching your dog to heel. Practice regularly and use positive reinforcement to encourage and reward your dog for maintaining the proper position. Gradually, your dog will learn to heel reliably during walks.

Common Mistakes and Corrections

❖Pulling on the leash

If your dog pulls on the leash, stop walking immediately and wait for it to return to the desired position. Reward and continue when it does.

❖Losing focus and breaking form

Dogs can become easily distracted during walks. Gently redirect their attention with verbal cues or treats to regain focus.

❖How to re-calibrate if your dog doesn't 'Heel' properly

If your dog constantly doesn't heel properly, revisit the foundational training stages and reinforce them. Consistency and repetition are essential.

The "Place" Command

The "Place" command instructs your dog to go to a specific spot, such as a crate, bed, or mat, and remain there until given further direction. It's a practical and versatile command for managing your dog's behavior in various situations.

You can use the "Place" command to manage your dog's behavior when guests visit, during mealtimes, or when you need your dog to be calm and stationary. It provides a designated safe space for your dog.

"Place" command also makes home life more manageable by giving your dog clear boundaries and expectations. It prevents jumping on guests, begging at the table, and other unwanted behaviors.

Picture a dog who knows the "Place" command. When guests arrive, the dog goes to its designated spot and waits quietly. During meals, it remains on its mat, ensuring a peaceful dining experience. "Place" enhances the dog's overall behavior and quality of life.

●Steps to Teach 'Place'

Teaching your dog the "Place" command is a valuable part of advanced training. Here are the steps to teach this command:

1. **Choose the "Place":** Select a specific location where you want your dog to go when given the "Place" command. This can be a mat, bed, or any designated spot.
2. **Prepare Treats:** Have high-value treats ready for rewards.
3. **Introduce the Command:** With your dog on a leash, lead them to the chosen spot while saying "Place." Use a treat to lure them onto the spot.
4. **Reward and Praise:** Once your dog is in the designated place, reward them with treats and praise. Use phrases like "Good place!" to reinforce the association.
5. **Extend the Time:** Ask your dog to stay on the spot for a few seconds. Gradually extend the time as your dog becomes more comfortable.
6. **Add Distance:** Once your dog is staying on the spot reliably, take a step away from them while they remain in place. Use the "stay" command if needed.
7. **Release Command:** Introduce a release command like "Okay" to let your dog know they can leave the place. Use this command consistently to signal the end of the "Place" exercise.
8. **Repeat and Increase Duration:** Practice the "Place" command regularly, gradually increasing the duration and distance you ask your dog to stay on the spot.
9. **Add Distractions:** Introduce distractions gradually to test your dog's ability to stay in the designated place. Start with mild distractions and build up to more challenging ones.
10. **Practice Consistency:** Be consistent with your commands and rewards. Use positive reinforcement to encourage your dog to stay in place.
11. **Expand to Different Locations:** Once your dog has mastered "Place" in one location, practice it in various areas to generalize the command.

12. **Review and Maintain:** Periodically revisit the "Place" command to reinforce your dog's understanding and maintain their skills.

Teaching "Place" requires patience and consistent training. It's a useful command for controlling your dog's behavior and ensuring they stay in a designated area when needed.

The "Off" Command

"Off" instructs your dog to remove itself from whatever it's on, such as furniture or a person. It's essential for teaching boundaries and preventing your dog from jumping on people.

It is especially useful when your dog tries to jump on guests, children, or when you want your pet to get off the furniture. It promotes respectful behavior and ensures safety.

Teaching "Off" also serves as a preventative measure to avoid accidents and discomfort. It's a courteous way to ensure that your dog interacts with people and objects appropriately.

●Training Basics for 'Off'

Teaching your dog the "Off" command is essential for preventing them from jumping on people or objects. Here are the training basics for this command:

1. **Prepare Treats and Leash:** Gather high-value treats and have your dog on a leash for control during training.

2. **Start with Basic Sit:** Begin with your dog in a sit position, as this makes it easier for them to understand the concept of "Off."

3. **Introduce the Cue:** With your dog on a leash, say "Off" in a clear and firm tone.

4. Use a Lure - While saying "Off," use a treat to guide your dog away from the person or object they're trying to jump on.

5. **Reward and Praise:** As soon as your dog's paws are off the person or object, reward them with a treat and offer praise.

6. **Practice Consistency:** Practice the "Off" command consistently, especially when your dog attempts to jump. The goal is to associate the word "Off" with the action of not jumping.

7. **Reinforce with Sit:** After saying "Off" and guiding your dog away from the object, ask for a "Sit" command to encourage an alternative, polite behavior.

8. **Gradual Improvement:** As your dog gets better at understanding "Off," start using it in various situations and with different people.

9. **Continue Reinforcement:** Be consistent in using the "Off" command and rewarding your dog whenever they respond appropriately.

10. **Ignore Jumping:** If your dog jumps on you or someone else, turn away and avoid giving them attention until they "Off." This helps them understand that jumping is not rewarded.

11. **Generalize the Command:** Practice "Off" with different people and in different environments to generalize the behavior.

12. **Be Patient:** - Teaching "Off" may take time, so be patient and consistent in your training.

With practice and consistency, your dog will learn to respond to the "Off" command and refrain from jumping on people or objects. This command is particularly useful for maintaining polite and well-behaved interactions.

Riley, a brilliant Border Collie, started her day with a tailored breakfast, prepared by her owner. After some agility training, she showed off her skills. She flawlessly demonstrated "sit," "stay," and "roll over." The highlight was her math trick – barking the square root of 16 on command. Then, she accompanied her owner to the office, where she executed complex tasks like fetching specific files and delivering messages. At the park, she played a game of "hide and seek," flawlessly finding her owner. Finally, she settled in the evening, executing her nightly routine with precision, from turning off lights to closing doors, leaving everyone in awe of her advanced canine abilities.

As we gracefully leap from the world of advanced commands, let's twirl our way into Chapter 4: The Art of Teaching Tricks, where the magic of canine comedy awaits!

4

The Art of Teaching Tricks

"Trick training isn't just for fun; it's a dialogue between you and your dog that enhances communication, challenges their mind, and celebrates their individuality."
— Kyra Sundance, renowned dog trainer, author of "101 Dog Tricks" and founder of Do More with Your Dog

* * *

The Role of Tricks

Tricks have that "wow factor," but their real superpower lies in giving your furry Einsteins some much-needed mental gymnastics. Picture this: your pup dons a tiny professor's cap, and instead of pondering the meaning of life, they're busy solving trick puzzles. That's right, trick training is like sending your dog to doggy Harvard, keeping their gray matter in tip-top shape and boredom at bay. So, while tricks might seem like showbiz, they're secretly fulfilling your dog's dreams of becoming a genius!

But wait, there's more! Tricks aren't just about preventing the dreaded doggy boredom; they're your secret weapon against destructive behavior. Think of trick training as your dog's version of a blockbuster action movie - it's thrilling, it's engaging, and it keeps them away from chewing your favorite shoes. Beyond the applause-worthy performances, trick training is the unsung hero of your dog's well-being, like a superhero saving the day in disguise.

In a heartwarming tale that should be made into a blockbuster movie, Bella, the therapy dog, proved that tricks can be more than just entertainment. She wasn't just a canine entertainer; she was a lifesaver in a fur coat. Bella's tricks weren't just for show; they were her superpowers. From recognizing signs of distress to fetching vital medication, she was a hero without a cape, proving that behind every great trick, there's an even greater dog.

An Engaged Dog is a Happy Dog

Let's talk about the doggy happiness equation, shall we? Mental engagement, my friends, is the secret ingredient. Picture a dog with a Sherlock Holmes hat, solving canine conundrums. That's mental stimulation in action, satisfying their curiosity and intelligence. You see, dogs thrive when they're mentally challenged, and that's not just a wild theory—it's science! Engaging activities, like trick training, are like brain workouts, promoting cognitive development and keeping stress and anxiety at bay. A happy dog isn't just about a wagging tail; it's about a mind buzzing with joy.

Dogs that ace trick training aren't just quick learners; they're the brainiacs of the canine world. By watching them master tricks, you're basically witnessing a furry Einstein at work. But here's the kicker: mental stimulation doesn't just make your dog clever; it could potentially make them live longer. No, I'm not pulling your tail; there's research to back this up. Mentally engaged dogs are like the Benjamin Buttons of the canine world, less likely to have behavioral issues, and with a lower risk of cognitive decline in their golden years. It's like the fountain of youth, but for dogs!

Mental Challenges vs. Physical Exercise

Okay, folks, gather 'round because it's time to talk about the ultimate doggy workout plan. It's a combo so powerful that even the Avengers would be envious—mental challenges and physical exercise. Picture your dog as a superhero in training; their mental challenges are like lifting weights for their brain, and physical exercise is the cardio that keeps their bodies in tip-top shape. It's a match made in doggy heaven, creating a canine powerhouse of well-being.

Mental stimulation through training is like giving your dog a Mensa membership. It engages their intellect and problem-solving skills, warding off boredom and the dreaded destructive behavior. But hold onto your leash, there's more! Physical exercise keeps your pup's body in prime condition, preventing obesity, and providing an outlet for all that boundless energy. The combination of mental and physical activities creates a harmonious blend, like a perfectly mixed doggy cocktail. Your dog not only thrives mentally but also gets to enjoy the physical benefits of exercise, all while keeping their superhero cape spotless. It's the secret to a fulfilled, happy, and well-behaved doggy companion. So, folks, remember, a happy dog is like a two-in-one combo - a mental gymnast and a physical powerhouse!

When it comes to scientific studies, well, they're like the wise elders of dog training. They nod in agreement, saying, "Yes, mental challenges combined with physical exercise are the way to go." Research shows that mental stimulation is as vital as a brisk morning jog for a dog's overall well-being. Experts stand on the rooftops and shout, "This holistic approach to training is the bee's knees!" It not only drains your dog's energy but also cranks up their problem-solving skills. The result? A dog that's over the moon with satisfaction, and an owner who's overjoyed with a harmonious pet-owner relationship. It's like a symphony of doggy well-being!

Building a Stronger Bond Through Tricks

Let's dive into the magical world of doggy communication, where tricks become the secret language you share with your four-legged friend. Teaching tricks isn't just about dazzling performances; it's about forging an unbreakable bond built on trust and understanding. Dogs are like eager students in a classroom, and trick training gives them structured lessons in the language of obedience.

Picture this: you're teaching your dog to "sit" and "shake." Through repetition, clear cues, and generous rewards, you're not just witnessing tricks coming to life; you're watching the birth of a deeper connection. This newfound understanding extends beyond the realm of tricks; it seeps into everyday interactions. Imagine the joy of seeing your dog respond to your cues with newfound clarity, creating harmony in your daily routines. Consistency is your secret weapon in this journey, and it ensures that your dog not only masters tricks but becomes a model student in all aspects of life.

● Shared Moments, Lasting Memories

Trick training isn't just a lesson; it's a shared adventure, like embarking on a quest with your loyal sidekick. Together, you and your dog unlock the treasure trove of trust and understanding. As you guide your furry companion through the intricacies of tricks, something magical happens. The dog learns to read your cues, and you discover the quirks, strengths, and hidden talents of your pet. It's a mutual effort that weaves a unique bond based on cooperation and communication.

The joy that fills the air when your dog masterfully executes a new trick is priceless. It's not just about obedience; it's a celebration of your partnership. You take pride in your dog's accomplishments, and they revel in your guidance. This shared triumph deepens your connection, and it's an emotional high that both of you will cherish forever.

Let me regale you with the tale of Max and Sarah, the dynamic duo. Max, the spirited Golden Retriever, and Sarah, his dedicated owner, embarked on a journey of trick training. From rolling over to fetching slippers, they conquered it all. One day, during a family gathering, Max pulled off a jaw-dropping trick. When Sarah playfully pretended to shoot him with an imaginary finger gun, Max played dead to perfection. The room echoed with laughter and applause, and Max's tail wagged in pure delight. It was a moment of shared joy that cemented the unbreakable bond between them.

● A Trust-Building Exercise

Teaching tricks isn't just about teaching tricks; it's a trust-building exercise of epic proportions. In this grand symphony of communication, every note is a cue, every reward is a crescendo, and trust is the harmonious melody that flows between you and your dog. As you teach and your dog learns, the bond between you deepens, and trust becomes the cornerstone.

Positive reinforcement is the heart of this trust-building process. When your dog behaves as desired and receives treats, praise, or playtime as rewards, they begin to understand the connection between their actions and positive outcomes. This, my friends, is the essence of trust. Your dog learns that when they look to you for guidance, good things happen. It's like a dance where you lead with fairness, patience, and clear cues, and your dog follows with trust and dependability.

To delve into the psychology of trust between dogs and humans, remember that trust in dogs is built on predictability, consistency, and a sense of security. Dogs lean toward owners who are fair, patient, and communicate clearly. It's a gradual journey of empathy and understanding, where the human-dog bond grows stronger and more mutually beneficial with each trick learned and every cue followed.

The Bridge from Commands to Tricks

Picture tricks as the fanciful castles of dog training, and basic commands as the sturdy bridges that lead to them. Basic commands like "sit," "stay," and "come" serve as the foundation of dog trick training. They establish a language of communication between you and your furry companion, laying the groundwork for obedience and respect. This foundation is like the trusty bridge that your dog crosses to enter the enchanting world of tricks. As they learn to listen to your commands and trust your guidance, they become more receptive to the allure of mastering new, captivating behaviors.

Sequential learning is the secret recipe here. It's the art of teaching dogs one step at a time, just like building a house brick by brick. Starting with basic commands and then gradually introducing more complex tricks allows dogs to develop skills and confidence methodically. Imagine teaching a dog like Max, who first learned to sit, stay, and lie down. Once he mastered these basics, he embarked on a journey to conquer more complex tricks like rolling over, playing dead, and even agility training. This step-by-step approach allowed Max to build a strong foundation of trust and competence. The case study of Max showcases how sequential learning, beginning with basic commands, paves the way for dogs to become proficient in advanced tricks.

● The Right Time to Introduce Tricks

So, when is the perfect moment to sprinkle some trickery into your dog's training routine? The answer lies in the mastery of essential obedience commands like "sit," "stay," and "come." These commands serve as the launchpad for your dog's journey into the world of tricks. Once your furry friend has a solid foundation in discipline and can focus on learning new and delightful behaviors, it's time to introduce some magic into their training sessions.

Age, temperament, and skill level are like the compass guiding your trick training voyage. Puppies are eager learners, but their attention spans might require shorter, more frequent training sessions. Older dogs may need extra patience and understanding, especially if their physical abilities are limited. Temperament varies widely; some dogs are born to be star pupils, quick to please and learn, while others may have a touch of independence. Tailor your training approach to your dog's unique character. Skill level, both yours and your dog's, plays a role in determining the complexity of tricks you can tackle. Beginners may need to start with the basics and progressively work their way up to the grand finale of advanced tricks.

While the ideal conditions for trick training may vary, there are constants that should never waver: consistency, positive reinforcement, and patience. And if you ever feel like you're navigating uncharted waters, don't hesitate to seek the guidance of a professional dog trainer who can customize your approach to match your dog's distinct needs.

● From Simple to Complex

Imagine trick training as a grand staircase with each step representing a new trick. Starting from the bottom, you ascend one step at a time, with each trick building upon the skills your dog has already mastered. It's like climbing the ladder of complexity, one rung at a time.

But here's the secret: don't rush your ascent! Dogs learn best when they're relaxed and engaged, so keep your training sessions short and sweet, typically no more than 10-15 minutes at a time. Remember that age, breed, and individual abilities play a role, so adapt your approach accordingly. Pushing too hard too quickly can lead to frustration and hinder progress. Always keep the atmosphere positive, using treats and praise to motivate and reward your dog for their diligent efforts.

When it comes to escalating trick complexity, think of it as a delicate dance. Introduce one new aspect at a time, whether it's a fresh command or an added twist to an existing trick. Practice consistently and gradually increase the level of difficulty. For example, if you're teaching your dog to "spin," start with a simple turn, and then, over time, add more spins or introduce a verbal cue. The key is to create a comfortable learning environment and celebrate your dog's achievements as they ascend the staircase of tricks.

Easier Than you Think

The Science behind Short Sessions

Dog training is a captivating realm that delves into understanding canine behavior and establishing effective communication with our furry companions. In recent years, the intriguing concept known as the "10-Minute Rule" has taken center stage in the dog training community. This rule proposes that concise, laser-focused training sessions, lasting approximately 10 minutes, can wield remarkable effectiveness in teaching and reinforcing behaviors in dogs. In this exploration, we'll embark on a journey through the scientific rationale behind these brief sessions, the philosophy of quality trumping quantity, and practical pearls of wisdom for seamlessly incorporating the 10-Minute Rule into your dog training repertoire.

Much like humans, dogs come equipped with varying attention spans. Puppies and young dogs, in particular, tend to possess shorter attention spans, while their more seasoned counterparts can muster prolonged focus. Nonetheless, even in adult dogs, the tides of attention tend to ebb after roughly 10 to 15 minutes. Hence, shorter training sessions harmonize more seamlessly with a dog's inherent attention span, making it less taxing for them to remain engaged and attentive.

The annals of scientific studies within the realm of animal behavior unfurl a fascinating narrative. These studies underscore the superior efficacy of shorter yet more frequent training sessions when it comes to the retention of learned behaviors. A notable study conducted at the University of Lincoln in the United Kingdom unveiled that dogs subjected to abbreviated, purposeful training intervals exhibited superior recall of acquired commands and demonstrated diminished levels of frustration or ennui compared to their counterparts subjected to prolonged sessions.

Esteemed figures in the dog training domain, such as the renowned dog behaviorist Cesar Millan, vociferously champion the merits of the 10-Minute Rule. Cesar underscores the profound impact of keeping training sessions succinct and focused, asserting that dogs tend to respond with greater enthusiasm when lessons are parceled into bite-sized, manageable portions.

Quality over Quantity

The crux of the 10-Minute Rule hinges upon the creed of quality reigning supreme over quantity. Amidst these fleeting sessions, dog trainers should ardently endeavor to ensure that every minute spent is a minute maximized. The training environment ought to serve as a sanctuary, devoid of distractions, and the trainer's unwavering focus should be lavished upon the canine apprentice. This intense devotion assures that dogs receive messages that are both lucid and unswerving.

Within the confines of a 10-minute training session, the delineation of precise objectives takes center stage. Whether the aim is to instill a novel command or reinforce an existing one, a well-defined target ensures that the training trajectory remains resolute. Furthermore, the doctrine of positive reinforcement be it through delectable treats or heartfelt praise, should be diligently deployed to promptly reward the manifestation of desired behavior.

Consider the tale of Shark, a spirited 2-year-old Labrador retriever.

His devoted owner, Sarah, grappled with the perennial nuisance of leash-pulling during their daily strolls. Sarah decided to embrace the 10-Minute Rule. Over the course of a mere week, David dedicated two succinct 10-minute sessions each day to leash training. He diligently worked on the art of loose leash walking, showering Shark with rewards for staying in close proximity and eschewing the urge to pull. Miraculously, within a mere seven days, Shark's behavior underwent a remarkable transformation, bearing testament to the accelerated progress that can be wrought through concise, quality training.

Practical Tips for 10-Minute Training

Embarking on a triumphant 10-minute training session unfurls with the canvas of an environment cleansed of distractions. Choose a tranquil, familiar setting that allows your canine companion to funnel their focus solely onto the task at hand. Any objects or stimuli that might beckon your dog's wandering attention should be gently ushered out of sight.

To faithfully adhere to the 10-Minute Rule, embrace the companionship of a trusty timer. This unwavering companion will ensure that you do not overstay your welcome in the realm of training, thereby preserving both consistency and the integrity of the rule.

Seasoned trainers ardently advocate for several supplemental strategies that serve as the cornerstones of a successful short training session:

- Single-minded focus: Concentrate your efforts on teaching or reinforcing a solitary behavior during each session. This strategic singularity prevents confusion and ensures that the training remains elegantly simple.
- End on a high note: Conclude your session with a flourish by

orchestrating a triumphant attempt, even if it necessitates breaching the 10-minute threshold by a smidgen. This leaves your four-legged trainee basking in a glow of accomplishment.

- Diversify rewards: Infuse variety into your rewards, oscillating between treats, praise, toys, or a medley thereof. This harmonious tapestry of rewards ensures that each session remains an exhilarating and engaging experience.

Breaking Down Complicated Tricks

Deconstructing a complex trick into manageable steps serves as the cornerstone of effective dog training. It commences with a crystal-clear comprehension of the ultimate goal. Let's embark on an illustrative journey: the endeavor to teach a dog the art of skateboarding. This formidable trick, initially daunting in its complexity, can be seamlessly subdivided into smaller, more digestible components. These include acquainting the dog with the skateboard, instilling a sense of balance, teaching the fine art of pushing the skateboard, and culminating with the exhilarating feat of riding it.

For dedicated trainers, this approach provides a meticulously structured road map, rendering the tracking of progress a breeze. From the dog's perspective, it serves as a masterstroke of canine psychology. By dismantling the trick into bite-sized portions, it minimizes frustration and ensures that our furry companions grasp each facet before venturing forth into uncharted territory.

Let's paint a vivid portrait with a real-world case in point. Enter Max, an exuberant Golden Retriever whose owner, Sarah, harbored the ambitious goal of teaching him to pluck a specific toy from a veritable treasure trove of playthings. With meticulous precision, Sarah employed the art of decomposition.

One Step at a Time

Guiding a dog along the path of discerning between toys and subsequently retrieving the desired one represents a progressive journey of heightened complexity. Here, the orchestration of verbal cues tailored to each toy assumes pivotal significance. Positive reinforcement in the form of rewards for a job well done proves equally indispensable. It's the quintessential approach that empowers dogs to unravel the intricacies of a task by understanding its individual components before embarking on the grand finale.

In the realm of dog training, positive feedback, delivered through the medium of treats and effusive praise, assumes a starring role. At each juncture, as our canine companion adeptly identifies and retrieves the correct toy, a cascade of treats and encouraging words rain down upon them. This symphony of positivity fortifies their grasp of the task at hand.

Allow me to regale you with the tale of D.O.G. (pronounced dee Oh gee), a dog whose journey was a testament to the power of deconstruction. As D.O.G. honed his skills, his joy and enthusiasm burgeoned in tandem. The sparkle of accomplishment that danced in his eyes when he flawlessly retrieved the designated toy underscored the sheer efficacy of this approach.

Piecing it All Together

Once a dog has achieved mastery over the constituent elements, the moment arrives to orchestrate their harmonious convergence, crafting the intricate tapestry of the complete trick. In Max's narrative, having become proficient at identifying and fetching an array of toys, he was beckoned to navigate the labyrinthine pile with a single objective: "Max, get your ball," Sarah would intone. Max, now a virtuoso, would deftly retrieve the ball from the midst of the playful chaos.

In this celebratory symphony of small victories, every successful retrieval by Max heralded a jubilant fanfare of treats and spirited play. This virtuous cycle of rewards kept Max ardently motivated, a willing participant in the grand finale.

Patience and consistency, as heralded by sage dog trainers, are the twin beacons lighting the path to success. Repetition and practice are the foundation upon which mastery is built. In the midst of these endeavors, the atmosphere must remain suffused with positivity and playfulness. Lastly, the judicious employment of a clicker, that precision instrument of reinforcement, can serve as the final flourish, sharpening the focus on correct behavior and underscoring the triumphant culmination of the trick.

Keeping Training Fun and Engaging

In the realm of effective dog training, the cornerstone is undeniably positive reinforcement. When you cultivate an atmosphere brimming with fun and encouragement, you lay the foundation for a bond that's as enduring as it is endearing. Just as humans thrive in a positive and uplifting environment, so do our canine companions. When dogs feel safe and joyful during training, they form an invaluable association between learning and happiness, enriching the connection between you and your furry confidant.

Here's the intriguing twist: dogs are remarkably perceptive when it comes to deciphering human emotions. They can discern your energy, mood, and even your body language. So, when you approach training with enthusiasm and excitement, your dog often mirrors that enthusiasm. Conversely, if frustration or tension colors your training sessions, your dog might respond with anxiety or reduced cooperation. Hence, it's imperative to embark on training with a positive mindset and a cheerful demeanor.

The stories of many dog owners attest to the remarkable transformations that unfold when training becomes a joyful activity. Consider the account of Sarah, the proud owner of a spirited Labrador. She reminisces about the shift in her once unruly pup's behavior when she infused elements of play into obedience training. "Instead of the monotonous drills, we turned training into a game of 'hide and seek.' Not only did it enhance his recall, but it also brought boundless joy to our sessions."

Mixing it Up

In the captivating world of canine cognition, novelty and mental stimulation reign supreme. Dogs thrive on the allure of new challenges and activities, which not only keep their minds fully engaged but also serve as a bulwark against the creeping specter of boredom, all while elevating their overall obedience. The palette of variety is rich and expansive, ranging from training in different locations to experimenting with fresh tricks and incorporating enticing props like tunnels and jumps. This variegation ensures that your dog remains a curious, excited, and thoroughly motivated participant in the training journey.

The art of balance takes center stage here, with a harmonious blend of easy, medium, and challenging tricks. Commence with those familiar, straightforward commands that your dog has already mastered – it's the perfect confidence booster. Then, gently introduce tasks of moderate complexity to tantalize their interest. Once these are effortlessly conquered, the time is ripe for the pièce de résistance: the more intricate tricks. The sense of accomplishment that washes over both you and your dog when they vanquish these formidable challenges is nothing short of exhilarating.

Seasoned trainers underscore the transformative power of diversity in training. Lisa, a certified dog trainer, extols the virtues of mixing things up: "A dynamic training regimen keeps dogs ardently engaged and perpetually excited. It's also the crucible where problem-solving skills are honed. I've witnessed dogs seamlessly transition from basic obedience to dazzling trick performances when training is a symphony of diversity."

Rewards Beyond Treats

Dogs possess individual preferences, and what might be a reward for one may fall flat for another. It's an exciting journey to explore various rewards beyond the realm of treats – think praise, toys, or spirited playtime. For some dogs, a belly rub or a spirited game of fetch proves more tantalizing than a simple treat. The key lies in uncovering what truly ignites your dog's passion and using it as a reward.

This voyage of discovery is a continuous odyssey. Pay heed to your dog's reactions during training – do they perk up more for a treat or light up when a game of tug-of-war is on the horizon? Over time, you'll decipher the code to your dog's heart. Armed with this knowledge, you can tailor your rewards to keep the embers of motivation burning brightly.

Consider the case of Indy, a tenacious Beagle who was somewhat indifferent to treats but possessed an insatiable appetite for play. His owner, Emma, recounts their transformational journey: "Once I recognized that Indy's heart belonged to play rather than food, our training sessions underwent a profound metamorphosis. We substituted treats with a beloved toy as a reward, and the results were astonishing. Indy became more eager to learn, and our bond grew stronger."

Popular Tricks

The Basics of Teaching 'Shake Hands'

Embarking on the journey to teach your dog to "Shake Hands" is a delightful endeavor in the realm of dog training. Here, we outline the fundamental steps to help you initiate this charming command:

1. **Prepare Treats:** Gather a selection of small, delectable treats to serve as rewards. Ensure your furry companion is sufficiently hungry and motivated to engage in the training.
2. **Get Your Dog's Attention:** Establish your training stage in a serene, distraction-free environment. Employ your dog's name to secure their attention and focus.
3. **Positioning:** Invite your dog to sit in front of you. This positioning facilitates their ability to offer their paw conveniently.

4. **Command and Gesture:** Utter the verbal cue "Shake" or "Paw" while extending your hand toward your dog's paw. Optionally, you can tap or gently lift their paw to encourage the desired behavior.

5. **Reward and Praise:** The moment your dog extends their paw, promptly reward them with a treat and shower them with praise. Positive reinforcement forms the cornerstone of successful training.

6. **Repeat:** Practice this command consistently. Exercise patience and avoid rushing the process. Initially, you may need to guide your dog's paw gently, but with time, they will grasp the concept and execute it independently.

7. **Consistency:** Employ the same command and gesture consistently during each training session. This consistency is crucial in helping your dog comprehend your expectations.

8. **Generalize:** Once your dog comprehends the command, broaden your horizons. Practice the trick in different locations and involve various people to generalize the behavior.

9. **Timing:** Precisely time your reward to coincide with your dog's performance of the desired action. This reinforces the association between the behavior and the reward.

10. **Limit Training Time:** Acknowledge that dogs have relatively short attention spans. Consequently, aim for several short training sessions rather than a single protracted one.

11. **Practice Regularly:** Consistent practice serves as the linchpin for reinforcing the behavior. Over time, you can gradually reduce the reliance on treats, emphasizing verbal praise.

Remember that every dog learns at their unique pace. Some may swiftly grasp this trick, while others might require more time. Patience, positive reinforcement, and the cultivation of a positive training experience are essential ingredients for success.

Common Challenges and How to Overcome Them

What to do if your dog is paw-shy: If your dog displays initial hesitancy about having their paws touched, consider gently handling their paws during regular petting sessions to desensitize them. Gradually introduce the "Shake" training into these moments to help them become more comfortable with the action.

Tips for phasing out the treat lure: While treats are indispensable for teaching the trick, it's prudent to gradually reduce treat dependency. To accomplish this, increase the number of times your dog must perform the trick before receiving a treat. You can also substitute treats with praise, petting, or a favorite toy as alternative rewards.

Advanced Variations of 'Shake Hands'

Elevate the "Shake" command by introducing your dog to advanced variations such as the high-five or a paw wave. To achieve this, adhere to the same training process as for "Shake," but encourage your dog to raise their paw higher, aiming for the high-five gesture. With consistent practice, your dog will become proficient in responding to this modified cue.

For those seeking an extra challenge, consider teaching your dog to shake with their non-dominant paw. This can be accomplished by replicating the same training steps but offering your opposite hand. It showcases your dog's impressive dexterity and intelligence.

Remember that patience, persistence, and a positive training environment are your greatest allies when delving into these advanced variations of the "Shake Hands" command

Common Challenges and How to Overcome Them

What to do if your dog is paw-shy

Some dogs may be initially hesitant to have their paws touched. If your dog is paw-shy, start by gently handling their paws during petting sessions to desensitize them. Gradually incorporate the "Shake" training into these moments to make them more comfortable with the action.

Tips for phasing out the treat lure

While treats are essential for teaching the trick, it's important to phase them out to avoid excessive treat dependency. To do this, gradually increase the number of times your dog needs to perform the trick before receiving a treat. You can also substitute treats with praise, petting, or a favorite toy as rewards.

Advanced Variations of 'Shake Hands'

Build upon the "Shake" command by teaching your dog to give you a high-five or wave their paw. To do this, follow the same process as for "Shake" but encourage your dog to raise their paw higher, aiming for a high-five. Over time, they will learn to respond to this modified cue.

For an extra challenge, teach your dog to shake with their non-dominant paw. This can be accomplished by repeating the same steps but offering your other hand. It's an impressive display of dexterity and intelligence for your dog.

118

Getting Started with 'Roll Over'

Embarking on the journey to teach your dog the delightful trick of "Roll Over" is a rewarding experience that can amaze friends and family. To help you get started, here's a step-by-step guide:

1. **Prepare Treats:** Gather a selection of small, delectable treats to serve as rewards. Ensure your dog is sufficiently hungry and motivated to engage in the training.
2. **Find a Quiet Space:** Initiate your training in a serene, distraction-free environment where your dog can focus solely on you.
3. **Basic Commands:** Prior to teaching "Roll Over," ensure your dog is well-acquainted with fundamental commands like "Sit" and "Down." This foundation is essential for the trick.
4. **Start with "Down":** Commence with your dog in a "Down" position. If your dog is not familiar with "Down," employ treats and gentle guidance to assist them in assuming this position.
5. **Lure the Roll:** Hold a treat close to your dog's nose and gradually move it in a circular motion toward their shoulder. The objective is to guide them into rolling over. As they follow the treat, their body should naturally begin to turn.
6. **Complete the Roll:** As your dog starts to roll over, persist in moving the treat in a circle until they accomplish a full roll. Simultaneously, use a verbal cue like "Roll Over" as they perform the action.
7. **Reward and Praise:** The moment your dog successfully completes the roll, promptly reward them with the treat and offer copious praise. Positive reinforcement forms the linchpin of effective training.
8. **Practice:** Repetition is key. Reiterate this process multiple times

during brief training sessions. Consistency and repetition are vital components.

9. **Generalization:** Once your dog comprehends the command, diversify your training regimen. Practice the trick in different locations and involve various people to generalize the behavior.

10. **Timing:** Precisely reward and praise the behavior at the exact moment your dog performs it. This reinforces the association between the command and the action.

11. **Gradual Fading:** As your dog becomes more proficient in rolling over, gradually reduce the use of treats. Maintain the utilization of verbal praise and occasionally reward with treats.

12. **Keep It Fun:** Training should be an enjoyable experience for both you and your dog. If your dog displays frustration or disinterest, take a break and return to training later.

Remember, not all dogs will learn "Roll Over" at the same pace. Exercise patience, employ positive reinforcement, and prioritize your dog's comfort and well-being throughout the training process.

To make tricks easier for your dog to learn in training, focus on clear communication and positive reinforcement. Break the trick down into smaller steps, beginning with the basic building blocks. For instance, when teaching "Roll Over," start with a solid "Down" command. Progress to luring your dog into a roll with high-value treats. As your dog succeeds in each step, gradually piece them together. This systematic approach simplifies the learning process and ensures your dog comprehends your expectations.

Additionally, establish a strong connection between the trick and a specific cue, such as a verbal command or a hand gesture. Consistency is paramount. Use the same cue during each request for the trick. Reward your dog promptly when they perform it correctly, reinforcing the association between the cue and the behavior. Also, diversify the rewards you use, including treats, toys, or praise, to maintain your dog's engagement and motivation. By practicing patience and maintaining a positive, reward-based training approach, you'll facilitate a more comfortable and enjoyable learning experience for your furry friend.

Overcoming Common Roadblocks

While teaching rolling tricks to dogs can be a delightful experience, there are common roadblocks that may require extra attention and creative solutions:

Lack of Interest or Motivation: Some dogs may not initially show enthusiasm for a rolling trick, especially if they don't perceive a clear benefit. To overcome this, enhance the engagement of your training sessions by introducing a variety of treats and toys. Experiment with different reward options to identify what genuinely motivates your dog. Sometimes, their favorite treat or toy can significantly boost their enthusiasm for learning the trick.

Fear or Discomfort: Rolling over can appear strange or intimidating to some dogs, leading to fear or discomfort. If your dog displays anxiety or avoids the trick, slow down and ensure they feel safe and secure. Revisit basic commands like "Down" to rebuild trust and work on the trick in smaller, more manageable steps. Gradually introduce the rolling motion while maintaining a calm and reassuring environment for your dog.

Physical Limitations: Larger or older dogs might encounter difficulties when attempting to roll over due to their size or joint issues. It's crucial to consider your dog's physical abilities and limitations during rolling trick training. If the trick appears too challenging or uncomfortable for your dog, explore alternative tricks that better suit their capabilities. The objective is to maintain an enjoyable and stress-free training process while allowing your dog to showcase their unique skills and talents.

Here are some common questions about teaching rolling dog tricks and expert answers to guide you:

Q: How can I teach my dog to roll over? A: Teaching your dog to roll over involves breaking the trick down into smaller steps. Start with a solid "Down" command, and then use a high-value treat to lure your dog into a roll. Be patient, use positive reinforcement, and practice consistently.

Q: What if my dog is not interested in rolling over? A: If your dog lacks interest, it's important to make the training environment engaging. Use enticing treats or toys to boost motivation. Sometimes, trying the trick in a different location or at a different time can reignite their interest.

Q: My dog seems scared when I try to teach them to roll over. What should I do? A: If your dog appears fearful, it's crucial to create a safe and reassuring environment. Start by revisiting basic commands and building trust. Slow down the training process and introduce the rolling motion gradually, always ensuring your dog feels comfortable and secure.

Q: How long does it take to teach a dog to roll over? A: The time it takes to teach a dog to roll over can vary widely based on the dog's age, temperament, and prior training experience. Some dogs may learn it in a few sessions, while others may take a few weeks. Patience and consistency are key.

Q: Can all dogs learn to roll over? A: While most dogs can learn to roll over, some physical limitations may make the trick challenging for certain breeds.

Next Steps and Advanced Techniques

Use 'Roll Over' as part of playtime or string multiple tricks together for a more impressive performance. Once your dog masters the basic roll, challenge them by adding extra rolls or speeding up the movement.

The Fundamentals of Fetch

Fetch is a timeless game that transcends the boundaries of species, turning even the most serious-faced dogs into enthusiastic athletes. Let's dive into the Fundamentals of Fetch with a canine twist shall we?

Selecting an appropriate object is crucial. We're not talking about throwing your favorite pair of socks; let's stick to a soft, lightweight ball or toy. Something that won't make your dog think they've just joined a canine dentist's obstacle course. Consider their size and breed – a Chihuahua might prefer a mini tennis ball, while a Great Dane is eyeing that giant rubber ball like it owes them treats.

And here comes the real brain teaser: some dogs are motivated by squeaky toys. It's like the canine version of a motivational speaker, only squeakier. Others are into toys that dispense treats upon retrieval, turning fetch into a gourmet experience.

Before launching into the game, introduce your dog to the basic commands. "Fetch" is the golden ticket, encouraging them to chase after the object. "Drop it" is your escape route from a game of never-ending tug-of-war. Treats are your secret weapon – trust me, dogs are like politicians; they'll do anything for a treat.

Now, picture Rex, the one-year-old Labrador Retriever, as our canine hero. Rex, full of energy and as enthusiastic as a dog at a squirrel convention, had never played fetch. His owner, Martha, decided it was time to introduce him to this Olympic-level game, but Rex was like, "Wait, what's fetch?"

Challenges

1. Rex's boundless energy made him the Usain Bolt of distraction during training.
2. The concept of fetch was as foreign to him as quantum physics.
3. Rex had a habit of treating the ball like a five-star meal, raising safety concerns and making Martha ponder doggy Heimlich maneuvers.

Training Plan

Martha, our dedicated doggy coach, kicked off with the basics – "Sit," "Stay," and "Come." It was like teaching a doggy version of the Macarena. In the following weeks, Rex got acquainted with the ball, learned to retrieve it, and grasped the concept of "Drop It." Training happened indoors and outdoors, with consistency and positive reinforcement as the MVP's.

Outcome

After seven weeks of training that would make even Olympic athletes sweat, Rex became the Michael Jordan of fetch. He could retrieve the ball from distances that left squirrels in awe, all while responding reliably to the "Drop It" command.

Lessons Learned

This case teaches us that patience is key, consistency is queen, and tailoring training to a dog's personality is the royal road map. Basic obedience training is the cornerstone of a dog's skill set, just like learning to walk before conquering the canine Everest. And remember, training should be a treat-filled joyride for both the dog and the human – after all, laughter is the best medicine, and in this case, it comes with a side of slobbery tennis balls.

Perfecting the 'Fetch'

If your dog decides to ghost the fetch game or transforms into a four-legged treasure hunter, fear not! Here's a pro tip hotter than a freshly baked biscuit: become the Beyoncé of the doggy world. Run away from your furry friend with all the enthusiasm of a squirrel at a nut convention. Throw in some excited jumps, make playful noises that would make a hyena jealous, and voila! Your dog will be chasing you like you've got a bacon-wrapped steak in your pocket.

But, oh dear, if they decide to play keep-away and drop the object somewhere in the Bermuda Triangle of your backyard, fear not, intrepid dog owner! Calmly ask them to "Drop it" as if you're a canine negotiator. Negotiation tip: treats are your diplomatic currency. Reward them when they comply, and soon your dog will think you're the Einstein of fetch.

Now, let's talk about challenging your dog because, let's be honest, a bored dog is a canine Shakespearean tragedy waiting to happen. Increase the distance you throw the object, but don't go full Olympian javelin thrower on your first try. We're aiming for a graceful Serena Williams, not an accidental satellite launch.

Gradually spice things up with directional cues like "left" and "right." It's like teaching your dog dance moves, but instead of salsa, it's the fetch cha-cha. "Left paw in, right paw out, you do the fetch and you shake it all about!"

And here's a scoop from our canine correspondent, Emily Turner, the dog trainer extraordinaire. According to Emily, "Perfecting the fetch is an art, like teaching a dog to moonwalk or recite Shakespeare. Patience and practice are key. Each dog is a unique comedy act, so tailor your training techniques to their stand-up routine. Increase the difficulty level gradually, and always shower them with applause... and treats, of course. Remember, fetch is not just a game; it's a stand-up comedy exercise for your dog's body and mind. Who knew laughter could be so fetching?"

Beyond the Basics

Now, let's take a paw-spective on Beyond the Basics and transform it into a tail-wagging tale.

For those seeking the Mount Everest of fetch challenges, gear up for the canine Olympics. Introduce multiple objects and watch your dog transform into the Sherlock Holmes of fetch, distinguishing between them like a furry detective on a mission.

And for the daredevils in the doggy world, there's the Frisbee Fetch – the Broadway of fetch performances. It demands improved accuracy and coordination, turning your backyard into a canine Cirque du Soleil. Add directional cues like "left" and "right," and you've got yourself a furry quarterback in the making.

Now, let me introduce you to the canine sensation that has the fetch community howling with admiration – Buddy, the Border Collie prodigy. Buddy doesn't fetch; he orchestrates a symphony of awe-inspiring brilliance.

Early Beginnings: A Natural Prodigy

Buddy's fetch journey began in the hallowed halls of puppy-hood. Imagine a fluffy Einstein with a fur coat – that was Buddy. His boundless energy and keen instinct marked him as a fetch prodigy, and his owner, Sarah, knew she had a four-legged Mozart on her hands.

Elevating Fetch to Art

From chasing balls to a ballet of acrobatics, Buddy's fetch evolution is a saga of agility, precision, and doggy genius. His repertoire includes pinpoint accuracy, handling multiple objects like a furry juggler, and turning every game into a dazzling display of canine prowess. The connection between Buddy and Sarah is a love story – a symphony of communication and trust.

Inspiring the Community

Buddy isn't just a fetch virtuoso; he's a community icon. Picture him participating in doggy fundraisers, captivating audiences with performances that rival Broadway shows. He's not just fetching balls; he's fetching hearts.

Buddy's Legacy

Buddy, the maestro of fetch, stands as a living testament to the extraordinary bond between humans and dogs. His legacy is more than just fetch; it's a love story, a tale of dedication, and an inspiration for dog lovers worldwide. Remember, folks, every dog has the potential to be a Buddy – all it takes is a sprinkle of dedication and a dash of love.

Tricks are fun, but what about when your dog's behavior is far from amusing? Let's dive into behavior correction, where we exchange the doggy stand-up for a little behavior therapy. It's time to unleash the wisdom in Chapter 5: Correcting Common Behavioral Issues

5

Correcting Common Behavioral Issues

"Correcting behavioral issues isn't just about changing a dog's actions; it's about understanding and altering the emotional states that drive those actions."

- Cesar Millan

* * *

According to the National Institute of Health, more than 80% of dogs kept in homes exhibit behavioral problems.

Why Dogs Misbehave

Let's dig into the root causes of misbehavior with a canine twist, shall we?

Lack of Training: Imagine being asked to follow a recipe without ever being taught to cook. Dogs feel the same confusion without proper training. It's not rebellion; it's just a canine shrug saying, "What do you want from me?" Consistent training is the key that unlocks a dog's good behavior.

Inconsistencies in training methods: Picture this: one day, you're told jumping on the couch is A-OK, the next day it's a no-no. That's the confusion dogs feel with inconsistent training methods. It's like changing the rules of the game midway. Can you blame them for a bit of rebellious streak? Consistency is the glue that holds the doggy rule book together.

Confusion from multiple human "pack" leaders: If you had five bosses at work, each with a different set of rules, you'd be sending out SOS signals too. Dogs thrive on a single boss, a leader, not a canine United Nations. Multiple leaders mean mixed signals, leading to a doggy identity crisis. It's not disobedience; it's a cry for leadership clarity. Unite the human pack for a drama-free doggy dictatorship.

Unmet Physical Needs: Ever had so much energy bottled up that you resort to stress-eating or redecorating your living room? Dogs feel the same when their physical needs are neglected. It's not defiance; it's the canine version of a pent-up energy explosion. Regular exercise is the doggy equivalent of hitting the gym – a tired dog is a good dog, and possibly a dog with fewer redecorating ambitions.

Diet issues affecting behavior: Imagine eating cardboard for dinner – not a delightful thought, right? Dogs feel the same about low-quality food. Nutrient deficiencies can turn even the sweetest dog into a less-than-happy camper. It's not misbehavior; it's a plea for better cuisine. Remember, a well-fed dog is a happy dog.

Medical conditions that could affect temperament: Imagine going about your day with a toothache or a persistent itch – not the most pleasant experience, right? Dogs misbehave when they're dealing with medical issues, and it's not a temper tantrum; it's a cry for help. Consult the doggy doctor before pointing paws at behavioral problems.

Emotional Factors: Ever had a bad day and just wanted to hide under the covers? Dogs do too. Misbehavior can be their way of expressing distress. It's not defiance; it's a canine emotional roller coaster. Positive reinforcement, socialization, and a bit of doggy therapy can turn that frown upside down.

Seeking attention through naughty acts: If you're at a party, and no one notices your new dance move, you might try a more attention-grabbing one, right? Dogs feel the same way. Mischievous acts are their version of seeking attention. It's not rebellion; it's a furry plea for a spotlight moment. Shower them with love, and they might stick to the simpler two-step.

Changes in environment or daily routine affecting the dog emotionally: Moving to a new house is like being in a sci-fi movie – everything looks different, and you have no idea where the snacks are. Dogs get it. Changes in their environment or routine are a real doggy emotional roller coaster. It's not misbehavior; it's a canine adaptation struggle. Stability, comfort, and a treat or two can ease the transition. Remember, even dogs need a bit of emotional support during life's twists and turns.

Behavior vs. Obedience

Distinguishing Between Behavior and Obedience

Let's embark on the whimsical journey of understanding dog behavior and obedience, where tails tell tales and commands become the canine ABCs.

What is Behavior?

Dogs, those furry philosophers, express themselves in a range of actions that could rival a Shakespearean play. From the dramatic sniffing soliloquies to the social interactions that could fill a doggy Oscars ceremony – it's a canine drama extravaganza. Picture this: a dog's world where fear is a brief cameo, excitement is a blockbuster, and curiosity is the never-ending quest for the Holy Grail of smells.

Now, let's talk instincts and learning. Instincts are the doggy genes kicking in, like the call of the wild or the irresistible urge to herd. Then there are learned behaviors – the canine scholars among us. "Sit" and "stay" are their academic achievements, while understanding how to mingle with other dogs is their social intelligence degree.

Aggression? It's the Hollywood drama, starring fear and dominance issues. Anxiety? Picture a canine Shakespearean tragedy with destructive chewing and excessive barking as the lead characters. And marking territory? That's their version of a graffiti masterpiece – "I was here."

Understanding these behaviors isn't just a crash course in Dog 101; it's the key to responsible dog ownership. Because let's face it, deciphering a dog's behavior is like navigating a canine Picasso – you need a guide to appreciate the masterpiece.

What is Obedience?

Now, onto obedience, the red carpet of canine training. It's not just following orders; it's their version of winning an obedience Oscar. Picture a dog in a tuxedo, confidently strutting their stuff in response to commands. Obedience is the language that bridges the communication gap between humans and dogs, turning our homes into well-choreographed dance floors.

Repetition, positive reinforcement, and sometimes treats – it's the doggy version of "practice makes perfect." Successful obedience training not only gives the owner a sense of control but also provides mental stimulation for the dog. It's the canine equivalent of a puzzle-solving adventure, keeping those furry brains in top-notch condition.

Now, basic commands like "sit," "stay," and "fetch" – they're the canine ABCs. Teaching these commands is like giving your dog a secret language, creating a harmonious symphony of owner-dog communication. Because in the world of dogs, knowing "sit" is like learning to say "hello."

Key Differences

Root causes and motivations
Behavior: It's the doggy diary of actions, from barking soliloquies to social escapades, driven by a mix of genes, experiences, and the occasional squirrel encounter.

Obedience: Think of it as a structured dance routine, motivated by the owner's expectations and the dog's need for a bit of discipline in their chaotic world.

Training methods applicable

Behavior: Positive reinforcement, counter-conditioning, and desensitization – it's the personalized therapy session for a dog's behavioral quirks.

Obedience: Clicker training, lure-reward methods, and shaping – it's the Broadway musical rehearsal for specific commands and behaviors.

Long-term and short-term approaches

Behavior: It's the epic saga, dealing with ingrained habits and reactions, requiring commitment and ongoing management.

Obedience: It's the quick dance routine, focusing on specific tasks and commands. Yet, like any dance, it needs the occasional reminder to stay in rhythm.

So, whether your dog is composing a tail-wagging sonnet or gracefully executing the "sit" ballet, understanding both their behavior and obedience is the key to a harmonious canine-human duet.

Understanding your dog's behavior is like interpreting a furry language with its own twists and tales. Let's dive into the canine behavioral wonderland, armed with treats, a keen eye, and a good sense of humor.

Identification: The Canine Detective Chronicles

So, your dog's behavior seems more mysterious than a detective novel. Signs of aggression, fear, anxiety, or barking that rivals a rock concert are your clues. It's a canine drama, and you're the detective in charge.

Note down these canine behaviors in your journal – the who, what, and why of their actions. Think of it as your dog's autobiography, written in barks and tail wags. Consulting experts is like bringing in the Sherlock Holmes of dog behavior – certified trainers and behaviorists. They're the Watson to your canine detective, conducting thorough assessments and offering solutions.

Treatment Plans: Canine Rehab and Medication Musings

Now, onto the treatment plans – the rehab center for your dog's behavior. Positive reinforcement, desensitization, and counter-conditioning are your dog's version of behavior rehab. They're learning to trade unwanted behaviors for treats and belly rubs – the Hollywood of doggy behavior.

Sometimes, it's like giving your dog a prescription for a challenging day. Medications come into play for severe behavior issues or when anxiety has turned your dog into a pondering philosopher. Consult your doggy pharmacist – the vet – for the right dose of wisdom.

Altering the environment is like redecorating your dog's life. Mental and physical stimulation, a consistent routine, and creating a safe, controlled space – it's the ultimate doggy Feng Shui. You're the interior designer, making their world a masterpiece.

Ongoing Maintenance: Canine Spa Days and Training Flexibility

Consistency is your dog's spa day. Reward and praise become the treats, affection, and verbal applause – the red carpet treatment for good behavior. It's like telling your dog, "You're the star, darling!"

Regular evaluations are your progress reports. Catching problems early is your preemptive strike against canine chaos. Think of it as your doggy parent-teacher meeting, where you discuss their latest tricks and escapades.

Flexibility in training methods is your canine yoga class. If one approach isn't working, try another. Adapt your strategies; it's the doggy version of "going with the flow." Seek guidance if needed – professional trainers are your partners for a well-behaved and happy furry friend.

Basic Commands

Embarking on obedience training is like teaching your dog the canine cha-cha – a dance of commands and cooperation. Think of it as laying the groundwork for a harmonious human-canine tango, where your pup becomes the four-legged Fred Astaire or Ginger Rogers of good behavior.

How to select the right commands for your dog

Choosing commands is like tailoring a canine wardrobe – not too tight, not too loose, just the right fit. "Sit," "stay," "lie down," and "come" are the little black dresses of obedience – universal and timeless. Throw in some extra commands like "chill" or "spin" to address your dog's individual quirks – the canine equivalent of a bespoke suit.

Rewards-based methods for obedience

Positive reinforcement is the doggy equivalent of receiving a gold star or a treat for a job well done. Treats, praise, and play become the canine currency, turning obedience training into a delightful game of earning rewards. It's like convincing your dog they're the MVP (Most Valuable

Pooch) in this training championship.

Progression

Once your dog has mastered the basics, it's time to crank up the difficulty like adding extra beats to the cha-cha. "Stay" transforms from a brief pause into a doggy meditation, and "heel" turns your pup into a disciplined dance partner. Complexity keeps their minds sharp, turning training into a mental workout.

Timing and consistency in training

Consistency is the canine metronome, maintaining a steady rhythm for your pup to follow. Timing is the symphony conductor's baton, signaling precisely when it's time to shine. With a consistent beat and well-timed cues, your dog will waltz through commands like a furry Mozart composing a masterpiece.

Socializing and real-world applications

Socialization is like introducing your pup to the VIP section of the canine social club – a place where they mingle, sniff, and paw-shake with other furry VIPs. Real-world applications take the training stage to the streets, parks, and family gatherings, turning your dog into the socialite of the doggy town.

Fine-tuning and Mastery

In the world of obedience, setbacks are like forgotten dance steps. Address them with the grace of a ballroom dancer – patience and additional training. Excessive barking is a temporary misstep, and leash pulling is just a fumble. With consistent correction and reinforcement, your dog becomes a master of the obedience dance.

For those aiming for the grand finale, dog competitions are like the Oscars of the canine world. Achieving titles like the Canine Good Citizen is your dog's acceptance speech, thanking you for being the paw-some director of their blockbuster training journey.

Common Problems and Solutions Barking Issues

● Understanding the 'Why'

Dogs bark like vocal virtuosos, each bark telling a tale – a potential threat, a desire for attention, or a canine soliloquy of boredom. To decode the barking opera, identify the triggers like a canine maestro pinpointing the key notes.

● Solutions for Barking

Teaching commands like "quiet" is like handing your dog a mute button for their vocal instrument. Positive reinforcement becomes the standing ovation, rewarding moments of silence. Consistency and patience are the encore, ensuring your dog's barking symphony stays melodious.

● Preventive Measures

Early socialization is the VIP pass to the doggy social opera, reducing anxiety-induced barking. A tired dog is like a doggy lullaby, less likely to compose a barking symphony. Establishing routines is the canine script, letting your dog know when it's time for a quiet interlude.

Chewing Issues

● Why Dogs Chew

Dogs chew like culinary critics exploring a new menu – a phase of puppy teething, an exploration of the world, or a stress-relieving binge. Each chew tells a tale, and your dog is the storyteller using their teeth.

● Solutions for Chewing

Chew toys are like the gourmet delights on your dog's menu – a feast for their jaws. Bitter-tasting sprays become the canine hot sauce, making items less appetizing. Obedience training is the chef's special, teaching your dog when to say 'no' to chewing. Positive reinforcement is the five-star review for making the right choices.

● Preventing Future Chewing

Puppy-proofing is the doggy home makeover, keeping valuables out of reach like precious artifacts in a museum. A tired dog is like a satisfied food critic, less likely to indulge in destructive chewing. Consistent behavioral training is the recipe for a well-balanced canine palate, addressing stress or anxiety through training and socialization.

These training tales turn your pup into the star of their obedience show, dancing, barking, and chewing their way to a well-behaved performance.

Types of Aggression

Dominance aggression

Picture your dog donning a crown, growling, and declaring, "This kibble is mine!" Dominance aggression is the royal decree of your furry monarch, asserting control over food, toys, and the kingdom of your living room.

Fear aggression

Imagine your pup as a furry superhero, cape fluttering in the wind. But when faced with a perceived threat, they morph into a snarling guardian. Fear aggression turns your brave superhero into a formidable warrior, ready to defend against the villains of unfamiliar faces and loud noises.

Territorial aggression

Your backyard becomes the fortress, and your dog, the vigilant knight. Territorial aggression turns your peaceful pup into a barking, lunging guardian, warding off intruders from their sacred land.

● Addressing Aggression

In the canine theater of behavior, positive reinforcement is the standing ovation. Rewarding good behavior becomes the treat-laden applause, encouraging your dog to play the hero, not the villain. Consistency and patience are the script, ensuring your pup becomes the star of their aggression transformation.

For more intense scenes, imagine a muzzle as the superhero's mask. It keeps the biting at bay while our hero learns the ropes. Seeking professional guidance from a dog behaviorist is like calling in the behavior superhero squad. They assess, strategize, and guide owners through the epic battle against aggression.

● Long-term Management

Ongoing socialization is the canine sequel, revealing the hero's growth from a loner to a team player. Exposing your pup to a varied cast of characters, animals, and environments turns them from a solitary warrior to a socialized superstar.

Behavioral modification is the canine screenplay rewrite. Techniques like desensitization and counter-conditioning transform your pup's aggression script into a tale of non-aggressive responses. It's the hero's journey from growls to greetings.

Monitoring for signs of regression is the post-premiere review. Even after the standing ovation, vigilance is the critic's eye. Signs of aggression may resurface like sequels, but with swift action, you can address these canine plot twists promptly.

And now, enter Dominic, the once-aggressive Pit Bull – the ultimate underdog story. Abandoned and labeled dangerous, he found a savior. With intensive rehabilitation and socialization, Dominic's fear transformed into loyalty. From aggression to therapy dog, his tale is a testament that, with a dash of patience and a sprinkle of love, even the most misunderstood dogs can become redemption's leading stars.

"Your dog is well-behaved at home, but what about when you're out and about? Time to explore socializing your dog in Chapter 6: Socializing Your Dog: The 10-Minute Guide"

* * *

Help Fellow Dog Lovers with Your Review: Unlock the Power of Sharing Knowledge

"Teaching your dog new tricks isn't just about making them perform for you. It's about the joy and bond that grows between you and your furry friend when you embark on this journey together." - Andi Dencklau

People who share their knowledge selflessly not only enrich the lives of others but also strengthen their own connection with the world. So, with that spirit in mind, I have a question for you...

Would you share your thoughts on a book that can help fellow dog lovers improve their training skills, even if you never got credit for it?

Who are these fellow dog lovers, you ask? They are like you— enthusiastic about training their beloved pets, wanting to make a difference in their lives, and seeking guidance to do so effectively.

Our mission is to make "10-Minute Dog Training Essentials" accessible to every dog owner. Everything we do stems from that mission. And, the only way for us to accomplish that mission is by reaching...well... everyone.

This is where you come in. Most people do, in fact, judge a book by its reviews, especially when it comes to learning how to better communicate with their dogs. So here's my ask on behalf of fellow dog lovers you've never met:

Please help those dog lovers by leaving a review for this book.

Scan or click here to leave a review

Your gift costs no money and less than 60 seconds to make a real impact, but it can change the lives of fellow dog owners forever. Your review could help...

...one more family enjoy harmonious moments with their furry companion.

　...one more rescue dog find their forever home.

...one more dog stay out of a rescue.

...one more puppy grow up to be a well-behaved, happy dog.

...one more pet owner feel confident and connected with their four-legged friend.

To experience the joy of helping fellow dog lovers and making their journey with their pets better, all you have to do is... and it takes less than 60 seconds... leave a review.

If you feel good about sharing your thoughts to help a fellow dog lover, you are my kind of person. Welcome to the club. You're one of us.

I'm that much more excited to help you strengthen your bond with your dog and enhance your training skills beyond what you can possibly imagine. You'll love the tips, techniques, and insights I'm about to share in the coming chapters.

Thank you from the bottom of my heart. Now, back to our journey of building stronger connections with our furry friends.

• Barking with gratitude, Andi Dencklau

PS - Fun fact: Sharing knowledge and helping others on their journey also enriches your own experience. If you know someone who adores their dog and wants to become a better trainer, send this book their way. It's a gift that keeps on giving, both for them and for you.

6

Socializing Your Dog: The 10-Minute Guide

" S ocialization isn't just about having a dog that's well-behaved around people and other animals; it's about confidently and comfortably being a part of the world."

- Ian Dunbar, renowned dog trainer and behaviorist

* * *

Buddy, a timid rescue dog, once cowered at social gatherings. Through patient exposure and love, his confidence grew. Gradually, he blossomed into the life of the party, wagging his tail, greeting everyone with joy. His transformation proved that with the right environment and care, even the shyest pup can shine.

The Importance of Socialization

Socialization in dog training is like sending your furry friend to Canine Charm School – the place where tails wag, and good behavior is rewarded with treats instead of gold stars. It's essentially their version of learning to shake paws and resist the temptation to chase the mail carrier.

Picture it as a pup's journey through Dogiversity – a prestigious institution where they master the art of "sit" and "stay" while resisting the urge to chase their own tail during exams. Forget doggy cliques; we're fostering positive interactions that make tails wag and ears perk up. It's like teaching dogs to say, "I'll sit for a treat, but I draw the line at rolling over for a belly rub during class."

Now, about introverts and extroverts. Just because Fido prefers a quiet sniff session over a raucous doggy disco doesn't mean they're antisocial. They're more into one-on-one woofs and cozy conversations. Let's debunk the myth that every dog must be the life of the paw-ty.

Dog socialization goes beyond human interaction; it's a symphony of sights, sounds, and smells. It's like introducing them to a four-legged universe of wonders – from sniffing lamp posts to conquering the mighty squeaky toy. Positive experiences turn pups into adaptable, confident companions. We're talking dogs strutting down the street like they're on a canine catwalk.

Components of Socialization

A well-socialized dog is exposed to a variety of people, animals, and environments during its formative months. Positive interactions with

146

diverse humans, including children and strangers, help build confidence and reduce fear. Encounters with other dogs and pets promote social skills and reduce aggression. Exposure to different environments like parks, cities, and homes fosters adaptability. Consistent training, controlled introductions, and positive reinforcement play crucial roles in developing a well-adjusted and sociable canine companion.

For instance, the socialization period in puppies is a crucial developmental phase that typically occurs between 3 and 14 weeks of age. During this relatively short window, puppies are highly receptive to new experiences, people, and environments. Socialization helps shape their future behavior and temperament.

Exposure to various stimuli, such as different people, animals, objects, and environments, is also essential for puppies to learn and adapt. Positive interactions during this period can lead to well-adjusted, confident dogs. Conversely, a lack of socialization may result in fear, anxiety, or aggression.

Things like puppy classes, supervised play dates, and controlled exposure to everyday sights and sounds also play a major role in their development. However, it's crucial to balance socialization with caution, as negative experiences can be detrimental. Properly managed socialization is key to raising a well-rounded and emotionally stable adult dog, ensuring they grow up to be friendly and comfortable in diverse situations.

Long-term, socialization lays the foundation for obedience, making training easier and more effective. In essence, early socialization is an investment in a well-adjusted and balanced canine companion.

Socialization vs Exposure

Socialization is more than a furry mixer; it's a crash course in doggy diplomacy. It's like teaching them the canine customs and dialects, turning them into ambassadors of the dog world. Positive reinforcement is their treat-filled passport to the land of friendly tail wags and belly rubs.

Forced exposure or 'flooding'? That's like making a dog binge-watch scary movies until they bark "uncle!" Not cool. Positive reinforcement and desensitization? It's the movie night with treats – a gentler way to modify behavior without traumatizing your furry friend.

Behavioral Advantages

Think of socialization as behavior therapy without the couch. Dogs exposed to the world's smorgasbord of experiences are less likely to unleash their inner drama queens. Reward-based methods are like the Oscars of dog training – with fewer speeches and more treats.

Statistics say unsocialized dogs might become the 'bark at everything' divas. Picture this: your unsocialized dog demanding a red carpet entrance at the vet's office. Socialized dogs? They're the calm VIPs who strut in with tails high, making everyone wish they'd brought treats.

Emotional Health

Socialization is the ultimate emotional spa day for dogs. Picture a shy rescue dog blossoming into a social butterfly, or an aggressive pup attending anger management through positive interactions. It's like doggy therapy, but with wagging tails and fewer Freudian slips.

Safety Concerns

Properly socialized dogs are the superheroes of safety. They're the caped crusaders of good behavior, ensuring harmony at the dog park and preventing canine conflicts. Imagine them as the neighborhood watch, barking at troublemakers but never resorting to paw-to-paw combat.

So, socialization isn't just training; it's your dog's passport to a world of tail-wagging adventures. After all, who wouldn't want their furry friend to be the James Bond of the doggy social scene?

The Right Approach

What is Positive Reinforcement?

Positive reinforcement in dog training is like giving your furry friend a standing ovation for their stellar performance. Imagine a world where every time you did something right, you were handed a treat, a pat on the back, or even a squeaky toy. That's the doggy dream we're talking about here. It's a method that involves rewarding a dog for displaying desired behavior. This can be done by providing treats, praise, toys, or other forms of positive stimuli immediately after the dog exhibits the behavior you want to encourage.

The idea is to make the dog associate the behavior with a positive outcome, which increases the likelihood that they will repeat that behavior in the future. It's a humane and effective way to train dogs, focusing on encouraging good behavior rather than punishing unwanted behavior.

Research in animal behavior science supports positive reinforcement, and let's be honest, who wouldn't be happier with a pocketful of treats? Studies have shown that dogs trained using this method exhibit lower stress levels and better overall well-being. A study published in the Journal of Veterinary Behavior found that dogs trained with positive reinforcement were less anxious and more obedient than those trained with aversive methods.

One success story is Puma, a fearful rescue. Positive reinforcement techniques, like using treats for calm behavior, transformed her into a confident and social dog. Puma's case demonstrates how patience and reward-based training can empower dogs to overcome their fears, showing that even the most timid pups can become shining stars.

Techniques of Positive Reinforcement

Positive reinforcement dog training is a bit like hosting a talent show for your canine companion, and boy, do they have talents! Here are some techniques that would earn a standing ovation:

1. **Clicker Training:** It's the canine version of pressing the applause button. Using a clicker to mark the exact moment the dog performs the desired behavior, followed by a reward. The clicker serves as a precise signal for the dog, like saying, "Bravo, Fido!"
2. **Treat-Based Training:** Who can resist a treat? Rewarding the dog with treats immediately after they exhibit the desired behavior. High-value treats can be particularly effective, making it a snack-worthy performance.

3. **Verbal Praise:** Dogs understand the language of love. Offering verbal praise, such as "good dog" or "well done," when the dog behaves correctly. It's like giving them a round of applause using words.

4. **Toy Rewards:** For the pup who lives for playtime, using toys as rewards is a game-changer, especially if your dog is highly motivated by play. It's the equivalent of winning a new game every time they get it right.

5. **Positive Interaction:** Sometimes, a good belly rub is all it takes. Providing petting, affection, and attention when the dog behaves appropriately. It's the canine version of a warm, fuzzy hug.

6. **Luring:** It's like leading your pup through a choreography of good behavior. Using a treat or toy to guide the dog into the desired position or behavior. Gradually reducing the lure as the dog learns the behavior.

7. **Shaping:** Dogs are natural performers. Reinforcing successive approximations of the desired behavior. This involves rewarding small steps toward the final behavior. It's like teaching them a routine, one step at a time.

8. **Capture:** Sometimes, brilliance strikes spontaneously. Rewarding the dog when they spontaneously exhibit the desired behavior without any prompting. It's like catching them in the act of being a good dog.

9. **Chaining:** Dogs can be choreographers too. Training a sequence of behaviors in which each behavior serves as a cue for the next, with a reward at the end. It's like putting together a show-stopping performance.

10. **Free-Shaping:** For the creative pooch. Allowing the dog to offer behaviors without any prompts and rewarding them for exhibiting the target behavior naturally. It's like giving them the freedom to express themselves.

Consistency, timing, and patience are essential in positive reinforcement training. The key is to reward the dog immediately after they perform the desired behavior to reinforce it positively. It's also important to use appropriate and motivating rewards based on your dog's preferences and to be consistent in your training approach.

Research by Dr. Sophia Yin, a veterinarian and animal behaviorist, and Dr. Karen Overall, an expert in veterinary behavioral medicine, has shown that positive reinforcement is associated with increased learning rates and reduced stress in dogs. It creates a strong bond between the dog and the trainer, as it builds trust and positive associations.

Common Mistakes in Positive Reinforcement

Over-treating or under-treating

Picture this: your dog's eyes gleaming with anticipation, expecting a gourmet treat, and you hand them a lettuce leaf. Some owners overdo treats, leading to obesity, while others under-reward, causing frustration. Striking the right balance is key. A study in the Journal of Veterinary Medicine recommends finding the optimal treat size to maintain motivation without overindulgence. It's like finding the perfect snack that keeps them motivated without the guilt.

Mistiming the rewards

Timing is everything, especially when it comes to rewards. Mistimed rewards can confuse dogs. If your dog is rewarded when they're not sure what they did right, they might not understand the desired behavior. Consistency in timing is crucial for effective training. It's like giving them a treat precisely when they hit the right note.

That said, positive reinforcement in dog training is a scientifically supported, effective method. Through case studies and a clear understanding of techniques, it's evident that with patience, timing, and consistency, dogs can be transformed into well-behaved, confident, and happy companions. However, avoiding common mistakes and misconceptions is vital to ensure the success of this training approach.

The Importance of Boundaries

Dogs, much like celebrities, need a set of rules to navigate the glamorous world of human homes. Setting boundaries is crucial for a well-behaved dog for several reasons. First, it provides dogs with a clear understanding of what behaviors are expected and acceptable. Without boundaries, dogs may become like unscripted reality TV—confused, anxious, or exhibit unwanted behaviors. Secondly, boundaries establish a structure that helps dogs feel secure and less stressed, as they know what to anticipate in their environment.

It's a move that complements positive reinforcement by offering a balanced approach to dog training. While positive reinforcement rewards desired behaviors, boundaries prevent or redirect unwanted behaviors. It's like having a script for the canine actor to follow, ensuring they hit their marks with finesse. This combination helps dogs learn and internalize proper conduct more effectively.

How to Set Boundaries

Setting boundaries for your dog is like creating a Marauder's Map for them to navigate different environments. Here are the magical steps for boundary-setting in various settings:

At Home

1. **Designate Specific Areas:** Think of your home as a magical kingdom. Decide which areas are the Forbidden Forest and use baby gates or closed doors to enforce these boundaries.
2. **Teach Commands:** Train your dog with commands like "stay," "leave it," or "off" – the spells to control their behavior inside the castle.
3. **Use Crates or Playpens:** Crates and playpens are like secret chambers. Use them to confine your dog when necessary, ensuring they stay within certain boundaries.
4. **Consistency:** Consistency is the wizard's spell. Be consistent in enforcing rules at home. Reward your dog for following boundaries and redirect them when they attempt to sneak into the restricted section.

Outdoors

1. **Leash Training:** The leash is like the dog's magical leash to your world. Use it to control their movements when outside. Train them to walk on a leash without pulling – a stroll, not a sprint.
2. **Practice Recall:** Recall is like the summoning spell. Teach a reliable recall command (e.g., "come") so your dog returns to you when called, even in the magical distractions of outdoor environments.
3. **Use Fencing:** If your yard is their Quidditch pitch, ensure it's securely fenced to prevent your dog from playing Seeker outside the boundaries. Regularly inspect the fence for any gaps or damage – no loopholes in this magical fortress.
4. **Avoid Off-Leash Areas:** In public spaces, follow leash laws like

the obedient wizard you are. Avoid areas where off-leash dogs are not permitted – no Room of Requirement for unleashed mischief.

Social Settings

1. **Socialization:** Socialization is like the magical diplomacy of the doggy world. Properly socialize your dog from a young age to ensure they behave well around people and other dogs – making allies, not enemies.
2. **Practice Obedience:** Obedience commands are like the spells of etiquette. Use commands like "sit," "stay," and "down" to control your dog's behavior in social settings – teaching them to be polite wizards.
3. **Supervise Interactions:** Be the vigilant wizard overseeing the magical duel. Keep a close eye on your dog when they are around other people or dogs. Be ready to intervene if necessary – no unruly wizardry allowed.
4. **Set Expectations:** Inform visitors and acquaintances of your dog's boundaries. Give them the magical rule book on how to interact with your dog – a spell-book of expectations.
5. **Positive Reinforcement:** In social settings, positive reinforcement is like the magical applause. Always reward your dog for good behavior to reinforce positive interactions – they are the stars of the magical show.

Remember, setting and maintaining boundaries is an ongoing spell. Tailor your magical approach to your dog's individual needs and the specific environment you are in. Positive reinforcement and patience are key components of this enchanted training.

Trevor, a dog owner, used gates to create magical portals separating her dog from her toddler's play area. With consistent use, the dog learned to respect this magical boundary, creating a safer environment for the child. It's like crafting protective spells for the ones you love.

Enforcing Boundaries Consistently

Consistency is the magical scroll in the wizard's library. Dogs thrive on predictability. Enforcing boundaries consistently is like keeping the magical contract intact – the dog knows what is expected, making it easier for them to follow the script.

One challenge is the temptation to relax boundaries over time. It's like lowering the drawbridge after the enemy has retreated – confusing for the dog. Inconsistent communication among family members is like having different magical languages. It hinders progress and creates chaos in the enchanted kingdom.

To avoid summoning the chaos demons:

- **Set Clear Rules:** Establish the magical decree. Ensure everyone in the household understands and follows the rules written in the Book of Expectations.
- **Use Positive Reinforcement:** Positive reinforcement is like the golden key. Reward dogs when they respect boundaries. It's like filling their magical goblet with treats for being noble wizards.
- **Consistently Correct and Redirect:** When mischief is afoot, consistently correct and redirect unwanted behaviors. It's like using counter-spells to steer the dog back onto the magical path.

In conclusion, positive reinforcement and boundary-setting are not just training methods; they are the magical spells that transform dogs into well-behaved companions. It's not about turning your dog into a mere Muggle but a wizard in their own right. So, embrace the magic, cast the spells, and watch as your canine companion becomes the magical creature you always knew they could be.

Socialization Exercises

Importance of Socializing with Humans

Meeting new people is like expanding your dog's social circle – the more, the merrier! It's a crucial act for a dog's emotional development, helping them build a trust network, reduce anxiety, and develop the social charm of a canine diplomat. Socialization is the ABCs of a dog's upbringing, especially during their puppy semesters. It's like sending them to the Hogwarts of experiences, exposing them to various sights, sounds, and humans, making them well-rounded pets.

Well-socialized dogs are the social butterflies of the canine world. According to the American Veterinary Society of Animal Behavior, dogs that undergo proper socialization in their early semesters are less likely to develop fear-based aggression or anxiety. A well-socialized dog is like a versatile Gryffindor, adaptable and comfortable in various environments.

Enter Terry, the once-fearful rescue dog. She was the introvert at the doggy party, cowering, barking, or hiding when guests arrived. Luna's owner, the wise doggy Dumbledore, knew that socialization was the magical spell Terry needed. With the guidance of a professional dog trainer, Terry gradually met people in controlled environments. She was like a student in the Defense against the Dark Arts class, exposed to various individuals, their voices, and movements. Over time, Terry's fear diminished, and she transformed into a sociable, happy pup who eagerly greeted new friends. It's like watching a magical evolution – from timid to triumphant.

Exercises for Human Interaction

Teaching your dog to sit when meeting people is like giving them a diplomatic stance – calm and controlled interactions are the goal.

Encouraging your dog to allow gentle petting is the equivalent of granting them the title of "Pettable Ambassador." It builds trust and positive associations with human touch.

Training your dog to make eye contact with you during interactions is like establishing a telepathic connection. It reinforces their connection with you, the wizard in charge.

When the time comes to introduce your dog to new people, take precautions:

- Use a leash for control – the magical tether connecting you and your furry diplomat.
- Monitor body language for signs of stress – it's like reading the magical runes of canine communication.
- Start with calm, well-behaved individuals – the Hogwarts professors of the doggy world.
- Avoid overwhelming situations initially – it's like easing them into

the Tri-wizard Tournament.

Bill, a previously aggressive Rottweiler, learned the "Sit and Greet" charm. Gradual, positive interactions led to reduced fear and hostility.

Betty, a shy Dachshund, embraced the "Touch" exercise. This helped her overcome her hesitation around new people and build confidence. It's like giving her a secret handshake for the doggy social club.

Overcoming Hesitation or Fear

Signs your dog may be afraid or hesitant

Watch for trembling, hiding, growling, or submissive behavior. Tail tucked, ears back, or avoiding eye contact are the doggy smoke signals of unease.

Tips on building confidence

Encourage positive interactions, use treats as rewards, and be patient. Gradual exposure and positive reinforcement are the magical potions here.

Enter Rocky, a rescue dog with severe fear issues. With dedicated training, he faced his fears through systematic exposure to new people. His owner, Sarah, used the outlined exercises, and Rocky transformed into a confident and outgoing companion, proving that patience and consistent effort can help dogs conquer their fears and hesitations.

Why Canine Socialization Matters

Having a dog that is social with other dogs is like having a companion fluent in the language of barks and tail wags. The advantages are numerous and magical:

This behavior has a profound impact on a dog's mental and physical health. It's like having a personal trainer for the mind and a fitness coach for the body. Socialization provides mental stimulation, relieves boredom, and reduces anxiety. Physically, it's the daily jog around the Forbidden Forest, maintaining a healthy weight and cardiovascular health.

Statistics reveal that well-socialized dogs tend to be the well-behaved Hufflepuffs of the doggy world. They are less likely to display aggression or fear towards other dogs or humans. A well-socialized dog is like a wand that adapts to various environments and is less prone to stress-related issues.

Dog-to-Dog Socialization Exercises

These exercises are the wizarding classes for dogs, offering structured environments for positive interactions. Controlled leash walking is like Defense Against the Dark Arts for dogs, teaching them to be calm around other dogs. Play dates are the doggy tea parties, allowing for friendly interactions, while group obedience classes are like the doggy version of advanced magical training, teaching them to focus a midst distractions.

160

While socialization is crucial, owners should be vigilant for warning signs, such as aggressive or fearful behavior. These signs indicate that a dog may need a break or additional training – a visit to the doggy Room of Requirement.

In a case study, Lucy, a previously fearful dog, was the Hermione of controlled socialization. Introduced to other well-behaved dogs in a controlled environment, her confidence grew, and she learned to play and interact positively. It's like watching a magical transformation – from timid to terrific.

Progress Monitoring

To monitor progress is like keeping tabs on your wizard's spell book. Observe your dog's behavior before and after socialization exercises. Document any positive or negative changes to understand the effectiveness of your magical efforts.

Utilizing a socialization checklist is like having a magical map. It ensures you cover essential socialization aspects, from exposure to various environments to meeting different types of dogs.

Gradually progress to more complex social interactions when your dog is comfortable. This can include visits to dog parks or participating in advanced training classes. Always prioritize your dog's comfort and safety – they are your magical companions on this journey.

Enter Barbie, a timid dog who struggled with socialization. Her owner was the dedicated wizard determined to help Barbie become a well-adjusted pet. They started with controlled leash walks, gradually increasing exposure to other dogs in a positive environment. Play dates with friendly dogs allowed Barbie to gain confidence.

The owner enrolled Barbie in group obedience classes, reinforcing her training and social skills. Over time, Barbie transformed from a shy, anxious pup to a confident and sociable companion. She thrived in canine interactions, showcasing the effectiveness of systematic socialization. Barbie's success story illustrates the magical journey from isolation to integration in the wizarding world of dog socialization.

Great, your dog is socialized. How about ramping things up with agility training in Chapter 7: Agility Training Basics?

7

Agility Training Basics

" C elebrate every small victory in agility training, for it's the journey of learning and growing together with your dog that truly matters."

- Sylvia Trkman, Renowned Agility Trainer

* * *

In Sweden 430 dogs participated in agility training. Number of disciplines performed by each dog varied between one and five.

Why Agility Training

Introduction to Dog Psychology and Physiology

Dogs, akin to wizards in their needs, have essential requirements for their well-being. Physiologically, they necessitate adequate nutrition, clean water, and shelter, with regular exercise and grooming playing pivotal roles. Psychologically, dogs thrive on social interaction, mental stimulation, and a secure environment. Emotional needs, such as love and affection, are equally paramount. Neglecting these facets can precipitate behavioral issues and health concerns. Thus, responsible care is indispensable for fostering a dog's happiness and health.

In the realm of dog training, the significance of both mental and physical exercise stands as an undeniable truth. Mental stimulation, encompassing activities like puzzle toys, obedience training, and problem-solving tasks, is pivotal for a dog's cognitive development, acting as a bulwark against boredom-driven behavioral issues. Simultaneously, physical exercise is critical for maintaining overall health and averting obesity, thereby curbing the proclivity for destructive behavior. A comprehensive training regimen, harmonizing mental and physical activities, not only elevates a dog's obedience but also nurtures a jubilant and robust companion, thereby fortifying the human-canine bond.

The Role of Agility in Mental Stimulation

Agility training, a veritable wizardry for dogs, presents an amalgamation of physical and cognitive challenges, engaging dogs in a dance of athleticism and intellect. This dynamic activity serves as a crucible for sharpening problem-solving skills as dogs artfully navigate obstacle courses. The exigency to process cues from handlers impels focus and teamwork. Memorizing the sequences of obstacles enhances spatial awareness. Beyond the physical exertion, agility fosters confidence, constituting a bastion for mental well-being. It is this blend of physical exertion and cognitive stimulation that propels agility tasks into the realm of activities that not only occupy a dog's energy but also foster a buoyant and active mind.

In a case study, Trent, a Labrador fraught with destructive proclivities, underwent a metamorphosis post agility training. Agility became the conduit through which Trent channeled his exuberant energy, fostering self-control and, consequently, mitigating boredom-driven tendencies. The structured environment of agility classes became the theater for imparting obedience and impulse control, resulting in a discernible reduction in destructive behaviors. This case underscores the multifaceted benefits of agility training, transcending the mere physical to significantly enhance the human-canine bond.

The Physical Benefits of Agility

The pantheon of health benefits offered by agility training is extensive and profound, akin to a magical elixir for canine well-being. Cardiovascular health, the citadel of a dog's vitality, witnesses improvement as rigorous activities elevate the heart rate, enhancing endurance and mitigating the risk of heart disease. Muscular benefits are equally substantial, with agility's repertoire of jumping, weaving, and climbing fortifying muscles, thereby augmenting overall agility and coordination.

The mantle of maintaining a healthy weight, a deterrent against obesity-related maladies, is shouldered by agility training. The ripple effect extends to mental stimulation, reducing stress and thwarting boredom. Beyond the physical realm, agility fosters a robust bond between the owner and the dog, thereby elevating their relationship into a sublime harmony. Furthermore, agility serves as a release valve for excess energy, curtailing the manifestation of destructive behavior. In summation, agility training emerges as a holistic approach to canine well-being, not merely tending to cardiovascular and muscular health but also contributing to the manifestation of a joyous and well-adjusted pet.

In a quaint suburb, the saga of Bumpy, a plump and lethargic dog, unfolded. Andrea, his concerned owner, embarked on a transformative journey by enrolling Bumpy in agility training.

The initially arduous odyssey, marked by huffs and puffs, gradually transformed Bumpy's physique. Agility, with its enchanting blend of physicality and intellect, not only assisted Bumpy in shedding excess weight but also infused a zest for life. The narrative of Bumpy and Andrea resonates as an ode to the transformative prowess of love, dedication, and a dash of canine determination.

Enhancing Obedience

Basic Obedience vs. Agility Obedience

The symphony of agility commands harmonizes with the foundational notes of basic dog training commands, forming a cadence that reverberates through the corridors of obedience and communication. Fundamental commands like "sit," "stay," and "come" constitute the bedrock for agility training, with agility commands such as "tunnel," "weave," and "jump" building upon these fundamentals. Agility training, in its essence, becomes a crucible wherein responsiveness to commands is honed, forging a robust bond and reinforcing obedience in the dynamic and challenging tapestry of the agility environment.

To fortify the interplay between agility and obedience, trainers seamlessly weave basic commands into agility courses. While statistical data might be sparse, the resounding acknowledgment within the community of trainers and enthusiasts attests to agility training's positive impact on obedience.

The Role of Positive Reinforcement in Agility

The maestro's wand in the realm of agility training is undoubtedly positive reinforcement, orchestrating a symphony of cooperation and camaraderie. This methodology, efficacious for various reasons, primarily forges a robust bond between handler and dog. The dog, akin to a virtuoso entwined in a harmonious duet, associates training with positive experiences, thereby enhancing communication and cooperation during the rigors of agility exercises. Furthermore, positive reinforcement becomes the pied piper, enticing dogs to perform desired behaviors willingly, driven by the prospect of earning rewards. In the realm of agility, where enthusiasm and a willing spirit are prerequisites for success, positive reinforcement stands as an invaluable ally. The repertoire of rewards, ranging from delectable treats to interactive toys, verbal praise, and the distinct click of a clicker, not only reinforces good behavior but also elevates agility training into an enjoyable and rewarding experience for the canine participant.

How Agility Improves Off-Course Behavior

The crucible of agility training, with its exacting demands for control, orchestrates an alchemical transformation in a dog's behavior, extending its impact far beyond the confines of the agility course. Agility, with its clarion call for focus, responsiveness, and precision, becomes a catalyst for improved communication between owner and dog. This heightened connection births a ripple effect, translating into enhanced behavior in diverse training scenarios. Dogs, tutored in the sanctum of agility, metamorphose into prompt followers of commands, rendering them more obedient and reliable. Moreover, agility's dual offering of mental stimulation and physical fitness becomes the antidote for excess energy, a potent deterrent against the manifestation of destructive behavior.

The teamwork etched into the DNA of agility training transcends the confines of the course, permeating into daily activities. This manifests in improved leash manners, a heightened recall response, and more harmonious social interactions with both humans and fellow canines. In essence, agility, akin to a sage mentor, inculcates discipline, confidence, and a resonant bond, laying the bedrock for improved behavior across myriad scenarios.

A tale unfolds with Pat, a spirited Labrador once given to wild escapades in outdoor settings. Frustrated by his unruly comportment, his owner sought the transformative alchemy of agility training. As Pat embarked on this new odyssey, a metamorphosis unfolded. The structured courses, demanding focus and coordination, sculpted Pat into a disciplined and well-behaved companion. Agility training became the crucible wherein Pat not only refined his physical prowess but also imbibed the virtues of obedience and impulse control. The once-wild Pat now heeded commands, maintained proximity during hikes, and greeted other dogs with grace. Agility training, akin to a sorcerer's wand, had molded Pat into a companion whose outdoor escapades were not merely enjoyable but truly harmonious.

Additional Benefits

Social Benefits

Agility training unveils itself as a tapestry weaving not only physical and mental benefits but also social advantages. It metamorphoses into a canvas wherein dogs are exposed to a myriad of faces and forms in a controlled setting, emerging as an efficacious tool for socialization. Through the crucible of agility classes or courses, dogs learn to navigate the terrain of collaboration with others, refining their social skills. The positive reinforcement embedded in agility training becomes a scaffold for building confidence, rendering dogs more at ease in the presence of new faces and novel situations. Furthermore, the dual offering of mental and physical stimulation serves as a salve for anxiety and hyperactivity, fortifying the crucible of socialization.

Building a Stronger Human-Dog Bond

The crucible of teamwork in agility transcends the mere acquisition of skills, emerging as a crucible for forging a potent and enduring bond between human and dog. In this high-energy symphony, effective collaboration becomes the linchpin. The interplay between owner and dog assumes the tenor of a seamless dialogue as they navigate obstacle courses in tandem. This constant interaction, akin to a finely choreographed dance, begets trust and understanding, elevating the relationship to a sublime zenith. As owner and dog work in tandem, anticipating each other's moves and adapting to each other's needs, a unique synergy unfolds. The shared triumphs and challenges become the glue that cements a deep and abiding connection. Teamwork in agility is not merely a pursuit of victory; it is a voyage into the realms of a powerful partnership with one's furry confidant.

Increased Confidence in Dogs

Agility training, with its crucible of challenges, emerges as a potent tonic for bolstering a dog's confidence. The very challenges that demand physical and mental acumen act as stepping stones for enhancing problem-solving skills. Success in navigating agility courses becomes a potent elixir, elevating a dog's self-esteem and fortifying the bond with their owner. The act of overcoming obstacles becomes a transformative rite, instilling a newfound confidence and enthusiasm for acquiring new skills.

The chronicle of Luke, a once-timid dog, stands testament to the transformative power of agility training. Enrolled by Susan in agility classes, Luke's journey unfolded from initial hesitation to exuberance. The once-reluctant participant leaped over hurdles, wove through poles, and navigated tunnels with zeal. Each triumph became a symphony of wagging tails and sparkling eyes, portraying Luke's newfound self-assurance. The tale of Luke is a parable, narrating how a leap of faith into the unknown realms of agility can lead to a metamorphosis, bringing forth the latent best in our canine companions.

In the expansive tapestry of a dog's life, the chapters of mental and physical exercise unfold as a saga of holistic well-being. From the foundational tenets of psychological and physiological care to the dynamic realms of agility, obedience, and additional benefits, each chapter stitches together a narrative of a harmonious and fulfilling partnership between humans and their canine confidants. In this symbiotic dance of care and training, the wisdom gleaned from each chapter becomes a compass, guiding both owner and dog toward the shared destination of a joyous and thriving companionship.

Getting Started

Dog agility training is like planning a surprise party for your pup. Picture this: your furry friend, maneuvering an obstacle course with the grace of a ballet dancer dodging party streamers. What's on the party agenda? Tunnels to zoom through, jumps to conquer, and poles to zigzag like they're avoiding party-goers.

By following the steps in this book, you and your dog can certainly have fun and build a stronger bond together. Of course there are always online videos for the DIYer as well. But, becoming a part of your local agility community is a huge benefit for you and your dog, so, feel free to reach out to me using the contact form at www.BorderColliePassion.com. I know a lot of great trainers across the country and would be happy to help connect you with someone in your area.

Understanding Agility Courses

Imagine a pup in a detective movie, navigating tunnels like a sneaky spy, leaping over hurdles with action-hero finesse, and weaving through poles like an undercover agent dodging lasers. It's not just an obstacle course; it's a canine adventure, a tail-wagging thriller!

In this controlled environment, it's not about solving crimes; it's about mastering agility equipment. Think of it as detective school for dogs—where treats are the detective's reward, and every successful hurdle conquered is a case cracked.

Creating a Training Schedule

Creating a training schedule is like planning a doggy fitness routine. Remember the 10-minute rule: because, let's be honest, dogs have shorter attention spans than a squirrel spotting a nut. It's not a marathon; it's a sprint—literally.

Consistency is the key to success, just like hiding treats in the same spot every time. Set goals, but don't expect your pup to become a canine gymnast overnight. It's a journey, not a race—unless there's a treat waiting at the finish line!

Safety First: Precautions & Equipment

Safety is priority number one, like having a lifeguard at a doggy pool party. Check equipment for wear and tear, so your pup's agility experience doesn't turn into a wardrobe malfunction.

Positive reinforcement is your secret weapon—treats, toys, and praise turn your pup into an agility superhero. And remember, even agility pros need a vet check; it's like a superhero health check-up.

Equipment Needed: From Jumps to Treat Bags

Setting up agility equipment is like preparing a canine playground. Jump bars become hurdles for your pup's Olympic dreams, tunnels transform into secret passageways, and weave poles are like dancing partners in a choreographed routine.

Treat bags, the Batman utility belts of agility training, keep rewards at paw's reach. Leashes and harnesses are like trusty sidekicks—keeping your pup in check until they're ready to go solo.

Optional but Helpful Gear: Clickers, Treat Bags, and Specialized Leashes

Clickers are the James Bond gadgets of agility training, providing precise feedback. Treat bags, the doggy fanny packs, are there for convenient treat access—because, in agility, timing is everything.

Specialized leashes, like magical lassos, give your pup freedom while maintaining control. It's like letting them explore Gotham City without causing chaos.

Where to Buy: Retailers Fit for Canine Royalty

Amazon, the kingdom of canine commodities, offers agility treasures for aspiring furry athletes. Chewy, the crown jewel of dog products, is your go-to for high-quality gear. Clean Run, the agility palace, specializes in equipment fit for champions. For budget-friendly shopping, sales and second-hand finds turn your pup into a frugal agility superstar.

Setting Up Your Training Space: Indoor vs. Outdoor

Choosing between indoor and outdoor training is like picking between a cozy reading nook and an adventurous camping trip. Indoor setups offer climate control, but outdoor spaces let your pup feel the grass beneath their paws.

Indoors, your pup becomes a homebody, safe from artificial distractions. Outdoors, it's a wild, uncharted territory—weather, real-world distractions, and all.

Size of the Training Space: From Cozy Nooks to Canine Kingdoms

Space dimensions are like choosing between a studio apartment and a canine castle. For beginners, it's a cozy nook—few obstacles, close together. Intermediate dogs get a spacious condo, with standard equipment. Advanced dogs deserve a canine kingdom, a vast space with complex courses.

Making Adjustments for Different Skill Levels: From Novice to Canine Prodigy

Adjusting for skill levels is like adapting recipes for novice cooks and master chefs. Beginners get a simple dish—few obstacles, low jumps. Intermediates face a more complex recipe—longer sequences and standard equipment. Advanced dogs whip up a gourmet feast—challenging courses, high jumps, and intricate sequences.

Remember, agility training is a canine carnival—fun, rewarding, and a little bit of magic. So, roll out the metaphorical red carpet, and let your pup shine in their agility spotlight!

Simple Agility Drills

The tunnel, a.k.a. the "doggy wormhole," is the VIP pass to canine agility stardom. Picture a long, fabric or vinyl tube — think of it as the red carpet for your furry superstar. Its job? Test and improve your dog's agility, speed, and, of course, their ability to make a dramatic entrance.

To avoid turning the tunnel into a scene from a canine horror movie (cue ominous music), start slow. Let your dog inspect the tunnel at their own pace, maybe even throw in a few treats to sweeten the deal. Positive associations, people!

● **Training Steps**

Teaching your dog to conquer the tunnel is like choreographing a four-legged dance routine. Here's your backstage pass to agility stardom:

Step 1: Gather Your Supplies

- You're the director, and your props include a dog tunnel, treats (cue applause), a leash, and a clicker or a "yes" for those who like a good verbal thumbs-up.

Step 2: Set Up the Tunnel

- Find a quiet spot for your dog's Broadway debut. Place the tunnel in a straight line or a gentle curve, because we're all about those graceful entrances.

Step 3: Introduce Your Dog to the Tunnel

- Imagine it's the first day of school, and you're the cool kid showing your buddy around. Approach the tunnel with your dog on a leash, let them sniff, and throw in some treats. Drama-free entrances only!

Step 4: Create a Positive Association

- Click or say "yes" when your dog shows interest. Treats rain from the sky. Life is good.

Step 5: Lure and Reward

- Hold a treat just outside the tunnel and do your best magician impression to guide your dog through. Cue the audience applause, and don't forget the treats.

Step 6: Gradual Progress

- Start with a short tunnel stint, then build it up. Positive reinforcement, patience, and treats — the trifecta of doggy motivation.

Step 7: Repeat and Practice

- Repetition is the name of the game. Practice for short bursts, daily or every few days. Treats and praise, people!

Step 8: Remove the Leash

- Unleash the star. Let your dog strut their stuff without the leash, but stay close for moral support and emergency treat distribution.

Step 9: Add Commands

- Introduce a dramatic command like "tunnel" as your dog perfects their routine. Timing is everything in showbiz.

Step 10: Add Variety

- Spice it up. Introduce curves and bends. It's like turning the tunnel into a Broadway musical, but for dogs.

Step 11: Stay Patient

- The doggy drama might need a few retakes. If your dog hesitates, hit them with more treats and encouragement.

Step 12: Have Fun

- Remember, it's all about the fun factor. Keep it positive, keep it enjoyable. Agility training: where tails wag, and treats flow.

Common mistakes to avoid during tunnel training

Agility training bloopers are a thing. Here's the gag reel:

1. **Pushing Too Quickly:** Trying to turn your dog into a tunnel aficionado too fast? Take a step back, Spielberg. Let them ease into it.

2. **Skipping Desensitization:** Tunnel phobia is a real thing. Desensitize your dog slowly. It's the key to a fear-free tunnel stroll.

3. **Using Negative Reinforcement:** Positive vibes only. Scolding equals drama, and we want a feel-good training montage, not a canine soap opera.

4. **Neglecting Positive Reinforcement:** Treats, treats, treats! Forget them, and your dog might decide tunnel time is overrated.

5. **Not Keeping Training Sessions Short:** Ever tried reading "War and Peace" to a dog? Long sessions are a no-no. Keep it snappy and engaging.

6. **Lack of Consistency:** Inconsistent commands are like changing the script midway. Stick to the plan, and your dog will hit their marks.

7. **Adding Distractions Too Early:** Too much background noise ruins the scene. Start in a quiet space before turning the tunnel into a blockbuster.

8. **Failure to Adjust to Your Dog's Pace:** Not all dogs are Oscar-worthy on the first take. Adjust your expectations, and let your dog steal the show at their own pace.

9. **Not Focusing on Safety:** Safety first, Spielberg. Ensure your tunnel set is hazard-free. We're aiming for canine stardom, not action movie mayhem.

10. **Skipping Basic Obedience Training:** Tunnel training is advanced stuff. Make sure your dog aced the basics before turning them into an agility superstar.

11. **Losing Patience:** Ever seen a director lose it on set? Not pretty.

Stay chill, and your dog will deliver an award-worthy performance.

12. **Overlooking Health Concerns:** A healthy star is a happy star. Check with the doggy doctor before embarking on an agility adventure. We don't want any unexpected plot twists.

13. **Not Reading Your Dog's Body Language:** Dogs are thespians with tails. If they're not feeling it, adjust the script.

By avoiding these bloopers and sticking to the script of positive reinforcement, patience, and consistency, you'll have a blockbuster tunnel training experience with your furry star.

Adding Challenges

To amp up the drama (cue suspenseful music), add challenges:

- Make the tunnel longer, because who doesn't love a grand entrance?
- Throw in some curves, like a canine catwalk.
- Test your dog's focus with strategically placed treats at the entrance. It's like hiding treats on the red carpet, but better.

Picture Bosco, once a tunnel-phobic pup, now an agility A-lister. With patience, treats, and maybe a canine acting coach, Bosco went from tunnel terror to tunnel triumph. Because in the doggy world, every tunnel has a silver lining.

Introduction to Weave Poles

Weave poles — the dance floor for dogs. These upright sticks aren't just decorations; they're the Beyoncé of agility training. Testing your dog's moves, coordination, and ability to follow cues, weave poles turn any pup into a dancing diva.

● Training Techniques

Training your dog to weave is like teaching them the cha-cha. Here's the paw-some guide:

Basic Introduction: Start with a single set of weave poles — your dog's dance partners. Begin with a treat lure, because every dance starts with a tempting twirl.

Gradual Progression: Like any dance routine, start slow. Add more poles as your dog gets their groove on. Consistent spacing is key, just like a perfectly choreographed routine.

Verbal and Visual Cues: Channel your inner dance instructor. Use verbal cues like "weave" or "poles" as your dog grooves through. Hand signals add that extra flair.

Positive Reinforcement: Treats, praise, maybe even a canine dance party. Reward your dog for nailing that weave routine. Positive vibes only.

Patience is key in the cha-cha of canine training. Some dogs are tango naturals, others take a little longer. Short, regular sessions beat a marathon dance-off any day. Celebrate those small victories and remember, it's a dance, not a race.

Weave Challenges

Turn your dog into the Fred Astaire of agility:

Speed and Accuracy: Crank up the tempo. Your dog isn't just weaving; they're dancing with the stars.

Obstacle Integration: Spice up the routine. Combine weave poles with jumps or tunnels. It's the agility version of a dance-off.

Enter Bravo, the Border Collie with two left feet (we won't mention that to him). Bravo's journey from pole-avoider to weave pole wiz was a slow dance of progress. With patient training, positive reinforcement, and maybe a hint of canine salsa music, Bravo mastered the weave, proving that every dog can be a dancing sensation.

The Role of Jumps in Agility

Agility courses, where dogs become airborne artists, defy gravity, and maybe audition for the next canine Olympics. Jumps, the acrobats of agility training, come in various forms — the high jumpers, the tire tango-ers, and the broad jump daredevils.

Pro Tip: Proper form is non-negotiable. We're not looking for Olympic-level flips, just some stylish hops.

Jump Training Basics

Training your dog to jump is like coaching them for the canine Olympics. Here's your gold medal guide:

Step 1: Gather Your Supplies

- Think of it as packing for the Olympics. You'll need jump bars, treats (the gold medals of the doggy world), a leash, a clicker, and a safe training area.

Step 2: Start with Basic Obedience

- No jumping the gun. Ensure your dog has nailed basic commands like "sit," "stay," and "come." Jumping is for well-behaved athletes only.

Step 3: Choose the Right Height

- We're starting with the bunny slopes. Set the bar low, or even on the ground. Confidence is the name of the game.

Step 4: Use Positive Reinforcement

- Treats rain from the sky when your dog does it right. A clicker or a verbal "yes" signals their acrobatic prowess.

Step 5: Lure and Reward

- Treats are the bait. Hold one on one side of the bar, and your dog becomes an instant high jumper. Don't forget the applause.

Step 6: Gradually Raise the Bar

- We're elevating the game, literally. Slowly raise the bar, maintaining that positive reinforcement. Gold medal, here we come!

Step 7: Repeat and Practice

- Like any athlete, practice makes perfect. Keep sessions short, enjoyable, and reward-laden.

Step 8: Add Commands

- "Jump" or "over" — your dog's cue for an Olympic-worthy leap. Timing is everything. A synchronized jump is a thing of beauty.

Step 9: Vary the Jumping Height

- Raise and lower the bar like a canine limbo. It's not just about height; it's about versatility.

Step 10: Vary the Approach Angle

- No one jumps straight all the time. Teach your dog to approach from different angles — the Michael Jordan of jumps.

Step 11: Safety First

- Helmets optional, but safety isn't. Check that the jump setup is stable and accident-proof.

Step 12: Gradual Progress

- Your dog is the gymnast; you're the coach. Progress at their pace. If they're not sticking the landing, lower the bar and rebuild that confidence.

Step 13: Maintain Control

- Leash it like a pro. Initially, keep your dog on a leash for control. As they become jump maestros, unleash the acrobat within.

Step 14: Celebrate Achievements

- Gold medals for everyone! Celebrate your dog's jumping triumphs with cheers, treats, and maybe a victory lap.

Step 15: Consistency

- Consistency is your golden ticket. Use the same commands and reward system. An Olympic routine is nothing without consistency.

Remember, safety first — no daring jumps without a safety net. Consult with a doggy Olympian trainer if your pup needs a little extra coaching. Agility training should be a celebration, not an injury waiting to happen.

Advanced Jumping Techniques

Take jumping to the next level, because why settle for bronze when you can go for gold?

- Practice jumps at different heights and angles. It's the doggy geometry lesson they never knew they needed.
- Work on your dog's stride and approach. This isn't just jumping; it's an aerial ballet.

Meet Drew, the Border Collie sensation of the agility jump world. Drew's journey started with low jumps, gradually reaching for the stars. His handler, Maggie, played the role of supportive coach, emphasizing safety and proper form. Drew's success wasn't just about winning competitions; it was a showcase of patience, dedication, and the magical bond between a dog and their handler. Now, Drew navigates agility courses with the grace of a ballet dancer, proving that with the right training, every dog can be a jump superstar.

Your dog is a little athlete now! But how do you keep them in top shape? Health & wellness is up next in chapter 8.

8

Health & Wellness Through Training

"Training isn't just about obedience; it's a journey to bonding, health, happiness, and wellness for both you and your dog."
- Andi Dencklau

* * *

Dog training is incomplete without an unwavering focus on health because a fit and healthy dog is not only a happier companion but also a more capable and willing learner, ensuring a harmonious partnership between you and your furry friend.

Nutrition and Training

The delicate dance of doggy dining, where proteins, fats, and carbs perform a gastronomic ballet for the well-being of our furry friends. Picture this: your canine companion adorned in a chef's hat, savoring a well-balanced meal, the epitome of culinary delight for the discerning palate.

Essential nutrients take center stage—protein for the muscle maestros, carbs for the energetic virtuosos, fats for the endurance aficionados and a symphony of vitamins and minerals for the overall well-being enthusiasts. It's not just a meal; it's a performance, ensuring your dog is in top form for the agility stage.

Foods rich in proteins, carbs, and fats become the canine energy sources, fueling their inner fire and sculpting their physique. Proteins, the prima donnas of nutrition, provide the building blocks for muscle growth and repair. Carbs, the prima ballerinas, pirouette as the primary energy source, gracefully fueling workouts and recovery. Fats, the unsung heroes, choreograph the dance of hormone production and energy storage. A balanced intake transforms your dog into a lean, agile artist, ready to dazzle on the agility course.

Now, let me regale you with tales of transformation! Imagine Star, the once-sluggish Bulldog, who, with a switch to a high-protein diet, found himself with newfound energy. He shed excess weight, a canine metamorphosis that propelled him into agility stardom.

And then there's Luna, the Border Collie, whose cognitive prowess soared with a balanced diet. Obedience became her forte, and she even mastered complex tricks. It's not just nutrition; it's brain food for the agility genius.

Lastly, we can't forget Rocky, the Labrador, whose joint struggles melted away with a nutrient-rich diet. His newfound mobility turned him into a top-tier athlete, proving that the right nutrition can be the ultimate game-changer.

Balancing Act: The Role of Proper Hydration

Enter the realm of hydration, where water becomes the elixir of life for our agile adventurers. Adequate water intake is not just a thirst-quencher; it's the secret sauce for temperature regulation, energy metabolism, and muscle function.

Hydration is the canine cool-down, preventing the dreaded heat stress and ensuring peak performance. It's the Aquarius of agility, the constellation of endurance, and the fountain of well-being. So, keep that water bowl handy—hydration is not just a necessity; it's the backstage pass to agility greatness.

To keep your dog hydrated during training, follow these tips:

1. Bring fresh water: It's not just a sip; it's a gulp of vitality. Always have a clean water supply available.
2. Frequent breaks: The intermission in our agility masterpiece. Pause for water breaks every 15-30 minutes, ensuring your star stays refreshed.
3. Use a portable bowl: The agility accessory that fits in your pocket. Invest in a collapsible, travel-friendly water bowl for those on-the-go hydration moments.
4. Monitor weather: The meteorologist's advice for agility aficionados. Adjust hydration needs based on the temperature, because even canine stars need climate control.
5. Reward with water: A sip as a standing ovation. Offer water as a reward for good behavior—hydration and applause, a winning combination.

6. Watch for signs: The canine semaphore for hydration. Keep an eye out for panting, excessive drooling, or lethargy—your dog's subtle cues for a water request.

7. Consult a vet: The agility nutritionist. If you're unsure about your dog's hydration needs, consult a veterinarian, because every agility superstar deserves a personalized hydration plan.

Common Dietary Pitfalls

In the grand feast of canine nutrition, there are cautionary tales, the Shakespearean tragedies of overindulgence and negligence. Beware, for the path to obesity is paved with overfeeding, inadequate portion control, and the siren call of low-quality commercial dog food.

Overfeeding, the Shakespearean tragedy of the canine world, leads to obesity and related health issues. Inadequate portion control is the Greek tragedy, causing malnutrition or the weighty burden of obesity. And the low-quality commercial dog food? That's the cautionary tale, the ghost story told around the canine campfire.

Let me share a tale of Boe, the canine gourmand. His owner, a well-meaning but misguided chef, consistently fed him table scraps and leftovers, disregarding the culinary masterpiece of proper dog food. The result? Boe faced severe digestive problems, obesity, and skin issues, a culinary tragedy that required a costly journey to restore his health. A lesson learned: dogs require a balanced diet, not just the crumbs of human indulgence.

Understanding Allergies and Sensitivities

Let's talk the canine masquerades of allergies, where disguises come in the form of itching, gastrointestinal theatrics, ear ballets, respiratory sonnets, and behavioral soliloquies. It's the Shakespearean tragedy of the canine world, unfolding in acts of discomfort and unease.

To unmask the culprit, embark on an elimination diet, a canine detective's quest to remove common allergens. Chicken, beef, grains—off with their heads! Consult your nutritionist, aka the veterinarian, before this culinary escapade. Transition your dog gradually, introducing them to a new diet over 7-10 days, a canine palate's gentle waltz. Keep a food diary, the memoir of culinary exploration, tracking progress and identifying triggers. Patience is the playwright, for it may take weeks to see the curtain fall on allergy symptoms. If needed, your vet may perform allergy testing, the canine quest for truth. Follow the vet's script for the best culinary drama.

The Dangers of Overfeeding

In the grand canine opera of agility, where leaps and bounds are the choreography, overfeeding and obesity emerge as the tragic characters. Excess weight, the cumbersome costume of canine performers, leads to reduced agility, strained joints, and a higher risk of injury during the grand leaps.

Obesity, the antagonist of our agility tale, exacerbates the potential for heat exhaustion, hindering the canine ability to regulate body temperature during the thrilling performance. Furthermore, overweight dogs face the perils of chronic health issues, the ominous specters of diabetes, heart disease, and respiratory problems.

To maintain the harmonious weight of agility dogs, the script calls for practical portion control and strategic exercises. Consult the canine nutritionist, the wizard behind the curtain, for the appropriate daily calorie intake. Measure food with the precision of a stage director, using a measuring cup for the culinary symphony. Implement a balanced diet, the musical composition of high-quality dog food with the melody of lean protein and harmonious carbohydrates.

How Much Exercise is Needed

Let's step into the canine fitness studio, where age, breed, and activity level are the choreographers of exercise routines. Picture your dog, the prima ballerina, leaping with joy or the laid-back loungers enjoying a leisurely stroll. The dance of exercise needs unfolds a canine waltz of energy and rest.

Age, the choreographer of the puppy pirouette, demands shorter, frequent bursts of exercise. Adult dogs, the seasoned performers, require a balanced daily workout. Senior dogs, the graceful swans of the canine world, may prefer gentler exercises, the ballet of the golden years.

Breed, the maestro of canine exercise, dictates distinct needs. The high-energy Border Collies and Retrievers crave rigorous workouts, while the Bulldogs, the lounge act of breeds, prefer a more laid-back routine.

Activity level, the tempo of the canine waltz, is the key. Some dogs are born dancers, naturally active, while others embody the slow jazz, lounging in the rhythm of their own beat.

Assessing your dog's exercise needs involves several factors:

- **Observe Behavior**: Watch for signs of restlessness, chewing, or digging—the canine SOS for excess energy. Conversely, if your dog seems lethargic or gains weight, it might need more activity.
- **Consult a Vet**: The agility consultant in the canine fitness studio. Your vet provides insights into specific needs, especially if your dog has health concerns or is a fitness newbie.
- **Experiment**: Try different routines and durations, the canine dance of trial-and-error. Regular walks, playtime, and interactive toys become the choreography of fitness.
- **Consistency**: Dogs are the prima donnas of routine. Provide a consistent exercise schedule, the symphony of physical and mental engagement. The 10-Minute Rule in Exercise

In the world of agility, where speed and precision reign, the 10-minute rule emerges as the avant-garde training approach. Picture this: short, intense exercise sessions, the Broadway of canine fitness, lasting just a few minutes.

This method aligns with the 10-minute training rule, the maestro's decree for brief but highly productive sessions. These short, intense exercises maintain engagement and motivation, preventing the canine yawns of boredom. More than just physical agility, these sessions boost cardiovascular fitness, muscular strength, and overall agility skills.

Incorporating agility-specific exercises into these short sessions becomes the doggy boot camp, sharpening responsiveness and enhancing navigation skills. The canine and handler bond, the love story of the agility world, strengthens as joy and efficiency intertwine. In summary, the 10-minute rule is not just a training approach; it's the choreography of a canine fitness ballet.

Risks of Overexertion

The cautionary tale of over-training, where the canine performers risk physical and mental burnout. The agility stage, once a realm of triumph, transforms into a theater of physical injury, mental stress, and the slow descent into decreased performance.

1. Physical Injury: Imagine our agile stars pushed beyond their limits, facing sprains, strains, ligament tears, and stress fractures—the ballet of pain.

2. Mental Stress: Over-training leads to canine anxiety, resulting in behavioral issues, reluctance to participate, and the phobia of agility equipment—the canine stage fright.

3. Decreased Performance: Paradoxically, over-training yields the opposite of agility greatness—fatigue, less responsiveness, and errors on the course—the canine fumble.

4. Burnout: Dogs, like thespians, experience burnout when subjected to excess training. Enthusiasm wanes, and agility becomes a chore—the canine disinterest.

5. Physical Health Issues: Over-training weakens the immune system, making dogs susceptible to illnesses. Chronic conditions like hip dysplasia or arthritis may lurk in the shadows—the canine health saga.

6. Loss of Bond: The tragedy of a strained bond between handler and dog. If training equates to stress, pain, or discomfort, the canine-human relationship unravels—the canine heartbreak.

7. Reduced Lifespan: Chronic over-training, the epic tragedy, leads to long-term health consequences, potentially shortening a dog's lifespan—the canine curtain call.

To navigate this treacherous terrain:

1. Listen to Your Dog: The canine oracle speaks through cues. If tiredness, soreness, or disinterest surfaces, it's time for a canine intermission.
2. Balance Training with Rest: The canine seesaw of activity and repose. Ensure adequate rest between sessions for muscle repair and mental rejuvenation.
3. Proper Warm-Up and Cool-Down: The canine ballet begins with a warm-up and ends with a cool-down. Incorporate these routines to prevent injuries.
4. Vary Training: The canine vaudeville. Mix up routines to stave off monotony and reduce the risk of over-training.
5. Consult a Professional: Seek the guidance of a canine fitness maestro—a professional trainer. Their expertise ensures a structured and safe training plan.
6. Regular Vet Check-ups: The agility health check. Have your dog regularly examined by a veterinarian to catch potential issues early.
7. Know Your Dog's Limits: Each dog is a unique performer. Understand their physical and mental boundaries and adapt training accordingly.

In the grand theater of agility, where leaps and bounds are the choreography, over-training is the villain of our tale. Remember, agility training should be a joyous and positive experience for both dog and handler. Striking the right balance between training and rest ensures your dog remains healthy, happy, and eager to showcase their agility prowess.

Excessive exercise can cast a shadow over our canine stars. Consider these real-life vignettes of dogs that suffered due to overexertion:

1. Working Dogs: The police and search-and-rescue heroes can be prone to overexertion. Stories abound of these diligent canines facing exhaustion, heatstroke, and joint issues from intense and prolonged duty.

2. Agility Competitors: While agility training is a thrilling sport, overzealous participation without adequate rest and conditioning can lead to injuries. Some agility dogs have faced ligament tears and joint problems from excessive jumping and running.

3. Marathon Running with Dogs: In a quest for canine marathon feats, some owners have attempted long distances without proper training. The result? Exhaustion, muscle fatigue, and joint stress— a canine marathon tragedy.

4. Sports and Hunting Dogs: High-energy dogs in activities like canicross or hunting can be pushed too hard, suffering from dehydration, heatstroke, and stress-related injuries.

5. Dog Racing: Greyhounds and racing breeds endure rigorous training and racing schedules, facing physical and mental challenges. Injuries and early retirements may be the canine consequences.

6. Competitive Fly ball: The fast-paced world of fly ball can take its toll on agility dogs. Injuries and exhaustion may be the price for overenthusiastic participation.

7. Hiking and Outdoor Adventures: Some dogs have been overexerted during long hikes or outdoor escapades, resulting in injuries or dehydration.

8. Herding Dogs: The herding heroes, if overworked without breaks, may experience physical strain and stress-related issues.

These real-life vignettes underscore the importance of responsible and balanced exercise for our canine companions. Dog owners must be vigilant, considering their pets' physical limitations, providing proper conditioning and ensuring that exercise routines are safe. Regular veterinary check-ups become the health surveillance, catching potential issues before they take center stage in the canine drama. The grand performance of agility is a collaborative effort between dog and handler, and maintaining a delicate balance ensures a standing ovation for a healthy, happy, and agile canine star.

Mental Health

Recognizing Stress in Dogs

Now, let's delve into the canine psyche, where stress unveils itself in a complex dance of behaviors and physical manifestations. Picture your dog as a stoic Shakespearean character, expressing stress through a unique canine soliloquy.

Behavioral signs take center stage—increased anxiety, the canine sonnet of restlessness, and the dramatic panting, an expressive canine opera. Submissive gestures join the performance, a ballet of cowering and averted gazes. And when the canine stage feels overwhelming, aggression or avoidance emerges as the tragic climax.

Enter Blond, the Border Collie, a canine thespian initially daunted by the agility stage. Signs of stress, like avoiding jumps and circling obstacles, marked her canine script. Yet, with a patient director, gradual training, and a crescendo of confidence-building, Blond's stress transformed into the triumphant saga of an agile champion.

Rocky, the Labrador maestro, composed his stress symphony through excessive barking and avoidance. His astute trainer deciphered the notes, identifying loud training arenas and unfamiliar canine faces as stressors. A change of venue, a controlled canine duet—Rocky's stress diminished, his performance reaching a harmonious cadence.

Common Stressors in Agility

In this grand canine theater, body language becomes the script, revealing the canine secrets of stress. Pay attention, for avoidance patterns and reluctance during training are the canine plot twists. Watch beyond the stage, into your dog's daily life, and unravel potential stressors.

To assist you, here are some theatrical tips for a canine stress-free production:

● Gradual Exposure: Scene by scene, introduce new elements with the finesse of a canine director, reducing the shock of unfamiliarity.

● Positive Reinforcement: Applause for desired behaviors becomes the canine standing ovation, building confidence with every well-executed cue.

● Calm Environment: The backstage tranquility, where training areas become peaceful sanctuaries, minimizing loud distractions.

● Short, Frequent Sessions: Act by act, opt for shorter, more frequent training sessions, preventing the canine encore of overexertion.

● Professional Guidance: The canine directorial maestro, experienced trainers, lends their expertise to identify and address specific stress triggers.

Agility as Mental Exercise

Imagine agility training as a canine Shakespearean play, a spectacle of mental stimulation intertwined with physical prowess. This mul-tifaceted activity engages the canine mind in a ballet of cognitive challenges and physical feats.

Dogs, the agile thespians, navigate a canine obstacle course, a Shake-spearean plot-line featuring jumps, tunnels, A-frames, and weave poles. They become the quick-witted protagonists, assessing surroundings, making split-second decisions, and dancing to their handler's cues. This dynamic process, the canine cerebral sonnet, keeps their minds sharp and engaged.

Problem-solving takes center stage as dogs plot their course through the agility narrative. Decision-making, the canine Shakespearean dilemma, unfolds as they choose between obstacles, considering speed, timing, and distance. Over time, this mental ballet enhances their ability to think and act under the spotlight of pressure.

Building Confidence

Agility becomes the canine confidence workshop, where dogs master obstacles and receive thunderous applause for their achievements. This symphony of overcoming challenges instills a sense of accomplishment, reducing anxiety and cultivating a more confident demeanor.

Take Lacy, the timid rescue protagonist, who, through agility's gradual progress, transformed into a joyful, self-assured companion. The canine narrative of confidence-building unfolded, proving that agility can metamorphose anxious dogs into poised, well-adjusted pets.

Similarly, envision Brody, a once-fearful pup, conquering jumps and tunnels to overcome his timid nature. Agility, the transformative force, allowed him to embrace courage, a canine evolution witnessed through the remarkable effects of this mental and physical ballet.

Creating a Stronger Bond

The agility stage is not just a platform for physical prowess; it's the forge where bonds between handler and dog are tempered. Collaboration and trust, the canine duet, weave a tapestry of unity and mutual understanding.

Sue and Draco, the Border Collie duo, epitomize an unbreakable bond sculpted through agility. Draco's trust in Sue's cues is the canine testimony to the deep connection that agility forges.

For James and Bella, the rescue dog, agility training was a transformative journey. Teamwork and shared victories solidified their bond, helping Bella overcome past traumas to become a joyful, confident companion.

Lastly, picture Brody, a dog whose life's narrative was altered by a balanced diet and regular training. Neglected and obese, Brody faced dire health issues. With determination, his owner introduced a nutritious diet and daily exercise. The once-lethargic dog shed excess weight, regained vitality, and embraced life with newfound energy. Brody's story underscores the life-saving impact of a healthy lifestyle, highlighting that a balanced diet and consistent training can be a lifeline for our beloved pets.

You're doing so well! Now let's put everything together in a 30-day training plan.

9

The 30-Day Training Plan

"Action is the foundational key to all success."

- Pablo Picasso

* * *

How much can a dog's behavior and skills truly transform in just one month with the right training techniques, dedication, and consistency?

The Plan's Structure

Week 1: Foundations

Behold the grand entrance of the "10-Minute Dog Training Rule," a canine ballet of brief, focused sessions designed to keep your pup entertained, educated, and ever so eager to learn. Picture it as a canine symphony where basic commands like "sit," "stay," "come," and "heel" take center stage, fostering obedience and safety. In a mere ten minutes a day, your canine companion embarks on a journey of positive reinforcement, improved communication, and a stronger bond with their two-legged maestro. It's the canine version of Shakespeare in the dog park, where consistency is the script, brevity is the key, and every bark is a sonnet of success.

To set the stage for this 10-minute masterpiece, create a canine haven—quiet, distraction-free, and filled with the melodious sounds of treats, clickers, and leashes. Establish a daily routine of short, focused sessions, beginning with the basics and gradually advancing. Positive reinforcement and rewards become the canine standing ovation, making the process upbeat and enjoyable. Remember, patience is the director's chair, and consistency is the backstage pass to a well-adjusted, disciplined companion. The 10-Minute Dog Training Rule: where time is brief, learning is vast, and tails wag in harmony.

Week 2: Building Skills

As the canine curriculum evolves, we enter Week 2—a symphony of skill-building orchestrated within the magical 10-minute time frame. Imagine your pup mastering advanced commands like a seasoned virtuoso, each cue a note in the harmonious melody of canine obedience.

Stay, recall, heel, place, leave it, and the life-saving emergency stop command—these are the crescendos of canine training. Short, focused sessions, the rhythmic beat, ensure effective learning and mental stimulation exercises, a dynamic counterpoint to physical development.

Consistency and timing, the unsung heroes of this symphony. Consistency, where commands and rewards follow the same script daily, creating predictability for your eager student. Timing, the maestro's baton, reinforcing good behavior with immediate rewards, a musical cadence that dogs quickly learn to dance to. Ten minutes a day, where attention spans are maximized, and the harmony of consistent, timely training is the sweet melody that echoes in every canine heart.

Week 3: Agility Training

And now, we step into the agility arena, a canine coliseum of fitness and mental acrobatics. Imagine your dog as a gladiator navigating tunnels, weave poles, jumps, and A-frames—the stage is set for a spectacle of coordination and responsiveness.

Basic exercises lay the foundation—weaving through cones, jumping over hurdles, and conquering tunnels. As the weeks unfold, complexity rises like a crescendo. Jump heights ascend, weave pole counts increase, and new challenges emerge, creating a thrilling narrative of agility and mental prowess.

Gradual progression, the guiding principle. Increase the difficulty over weeks, monitor comfort levels, and ensure a training experience that's both rewarding and safe. It's a canine ballet of fitness and finesse, where each leap and twirl strengthens the bond between handler and athlete.

Week 4: Tricks and Fun

In this final act, the stage transforms into a playground of tricks and delights, a canine carnival where "roll over," "play dead," and "high five" become the stars of the show. Positive reinforcement, treats, and praise—the orchestration of fun and learning.

Each trick, a choreographed dance, stimulates your dog's mental and physical agility. With patience and consistency, one trick at a time, witness the evolution of your canine companion into a skilled performer.

Celebrate their achievements, for every milestone is a victory deserving of a grand finale. Throw a little party, shower them with treats, and let the applause of praise be the crescendo that echoes through the canine halls.

Daily Goals Each day, a new theme unfolds, a canine calendar of focus and fun:

● Monday: Mastery

Monday As the curtain rises on the week, dedicate Mondays to perfecting fundamental commands. "Sit," "stay," or "come" take center stage, and precision becomes the guiding star. Gradually raise the difficulty level, challenging your pup's skills and turning each Monday into a mastery showcase.

● Tuesday: Trickster

The stage transforms on Tuesdays into a whimsical wonderland of tricks. Introduce new ones or polish existing ones like "roll over" and "shake hands." It's not just about obedience; it's about a mental symphony that enhances your pup's repertoire of delightful tricks.

● Wednesday: Agility Wednesday

Midweek heralds Agility Wednesday, a day to engage in the physical poetry of agility training. Start with simple drills, weaving between legs or jumping over low obstacles. As weeks progress, introduce agility equipment, creating a harmony of physical fitness and coordinated movements.

● Thursday: Thinker Thursday

On Thursdays, exercise your pup's mental prowess. Challenge their problem-solving abilities with puzzle toys or hide-and-seek games. Teach complex commands or introduce interactive treat-dispensing toys, creating a mental tapestry that keeps them engaged and sharp.

● Friday: Fun Friday

Fridays are a break from structured training, a day dedicated to enjoyable activities and bonding. Play games, go for nature walks, or try a new trick that adds both fun and mental stimulation to the repertoire. It's a joyous celebration of the bond you share.

● Saturday: Skills Saturday

As the week winds down, Saturdays are reserved for refining advanced commands—ones crucial for safety or public behavior. "Heel" and "leave it" take the spotlight, requiring more patience and practice. Ensure your pup's understanding and responsiveness to these essential cues.

● Sunday: Celebration Sunday

The curtain falls on the week with Celebration Sunday. Reflect on the progress and achievements, celebrating your pup's efforts with extra playtime and treats. It's a day to reinforce good behavior, applaud the milestones, and set the stage for another week of delightful canine performances.

Implementing the 10-Minute Rule

Welcome to the backstage of the 10-Minute Dog Training Rule—a 30-day extravaganza where canine stars are born, and tails wag in harmony. Applying this rule to your training plan is not just effective; it's a masterpiece in the making. Here's your script for success:

● Daily Sessions: Picture each day as a scene in the canine theater, where you dedicate at least one 10-minute session to training. These short, focused bursts are the secret sauce, more beneficial than the longest, most epic training sagas.

● Consistency is Key: Imagine consistency as the spotlight that never wavers. Stick to the same time each day for training, creating a rhythm your dog can dance to. Consistency turns anticipation into participation.

● Command Rotation: Behold the changing acts over the 30 days—a rotation of commands and exercises, each a stepping stone to greatness. Start with the basics, then weave in complexity like a plot twist that keeps your dog engaged and the audience (you) on the edge of their seat.

● Build on Success: As your dog turns into a training virtuoso, don't stop there—layer on additional commands and challenges. Each success is a standing ovation, and you're the conductor orchestrating the symphony of your dog's newfound skills.

● Positive Reinforcement: Every good performance deserves an encore. Always use positive reinforcement—treats, praise, and play—to motivate and reward your dog's efforts. It's the standing ovation that keeps the show going.

Scheduled Rest Days But even Broadway has its intermissions. In this canine theater, rest days are the intermissions that prevent overexertion and keep enthusiasm at its peak. Here's your guide to planning them:

● Frequency: In the 30-day script, include a rest day every 3 to 4 days. It's the pause that refreshes, ensuring your dog doesn't feel like they're in a never-ending encore.

● Active Rest: On rest days, the stage is set for low-intensity activities—leisurely walks, gentle play, or perhaps just some quality relaxation time together. It's the behind-the-scenes magic that keeps the show running smoothly.

● Recovery: Rest days aren't just breaks; they're the rejuvenation periods. They allow your dog's body and mind to recover, ensuring they're physically and mentally fresh for the next grand performance.

Weekly Check-Ins

Now, let's talk about the reviews and ratings of this canine blockbuster. Conduct weekly check-ins to track your dog's progress effectively. Here's your guide:

● Record Keeping: Imagine your training journal as the script of this 30-day epic. Document each session's details—the commands practiced, your dog's responses, and any challenges faced. It's the backstage pass to understanding your dog's journey.

● Behavioral Observations: As the director, observe the actors. Note any changes in your dog's behavior and attitude. Look for signs of improved obedience, increased enthusiasm, and reduced stress. It's the subtle cues that tell the tale.

● Performance Metrics: If your script includes specific feats—agility, tricks, or advanced commands—measure them. This quantifiable data is your box office revenue, gauging the success of your canine blockbuster.

But what's a blockbuster without a few plot twists? During your weekly check-ins, be prepared to make adjustments to your training plan. Here's your guide:

● Assessing Challenges: Identify the recurring challenges or roadblocks in your training sessions. Is there a scene your dog struggles with? Signs of fatigue in the canine actors? It's time to address them.

● Flexibility: Every great director knows the importance of flexibility. If certain exercises aren't working well, consider replacing them with more suitable ones. It's the art of adaptation.

● Progress Evaluation: Reflect on your dog's overall progress. Are they achieving the desired results? Are they engaged and motivated, or do adjustments need to be made to maintain their interest? It's the critical review that shapes the next act.

● Reinforcement Strategies: Like refining your script, assess the effectiveness of your positive reinforcement techniques. Ensure that rewards remain enticing and you're using them consistently. It's the magic wand that keeps the magic alive.

In a stunning 30-day transformation, Bailey, the once-unruly Labrador, took center stage in a training spectacle. With a dedicated owner and consistent training, Bailey mastered the art of obedience and leash manners. A calm and obedient performance replaced the tumultuous barking and destructive behaviors. The bond between Bailey and his owner grew stronger as they practiced together daily. Bailey transformed from a mischievous pup to a well-behaved and content companion in just one month. This success story highlights the incredible potential of effective dog training—a tale of triumph that echoes in every bark, proving that even the most challenging dogs can achieve remarkable progress in a short time with the right approach.

You've got the plan, but how do you stay motivated and make this a lifelong habit? That's next in chapter 10.

10

Making It a Lifelong Habit

"Training your dog isn't just about teaching them tricks; it's about creating a lifelong bond built on trust, communication, and understanding. Consistency in training is the key to a well-behaved and happy companion for years to come."

- Andi Dencklau

Regular dog training yields life-changing benefits by fostering obedience, reducing behavioral issues, enhancing safety, and strengthening the bond between pet and owner. It ensures a well-adjusted, happy, and cooperative canine companion, making every day a pleasure for both the dog and their human.

The Psychology of Habits

Ever wondered what's cooking in the intricate cauldron of a dog's mind when habits are brewing? It's a process called associative learning, a canine symphony where cues, actions, and rewards perform a harmonious dance. Picture it as a furry version of classical conditioning. The maestro behind the scenes? Dopamine, our four-legged virtuoso's neurotransmitter extraordinaire, playing the tune of repeat after me. As the pup links cues with rewards on a loop, voilà! A habit is born, prancing through the neural pathways.

In the grand theater of dog training, we unveil the Habit Loop, inspired by the maestro Charles Duhigg. Behold its three pillars: cue, routine, and reward.

- **The "cue"**: A spotlight moment, the cue is the doggy diva's signal to shine. "Sit," it commands, a common cue for the poised posterior descent.
- **The "routine"**: The main act, the routine is the canine choreography—sitting down in response to the majestic cue.
- **The "reward"**: Applause, please! The reward, whether it's a treat, praise, or playtime, echoes through the theater, sealing the loop with a paw-sitive note.

By orchestrating these components with precision, you metamorphose your dog into a virtuoso of good behavior.

Habitual Behaviors in Dogs: A Canine Cabaret

Dogs, our furry virtuosos, don't just stumble upon habits; they curate them through a mix tape of genetics, early socialization, and environmental beats.

1. **Barking:** The canine orchestra, expressing everything from communication to boredom. Excessive barking? Cue the training maestro!

2. **Chewing:** Puppies' teething symphony, with furniture as the unsuspecting percussion. Redirect the melody with appropriate chew toys.
3. **Digging:** Dogs, the landscapers of the canine world, dig for reasons aplenty. Training steps in to create a harmonious garden.
4. **Leash Pulling:** The leash, a tempting tango partner for many dogs. Leash training: teaching them the art of a leash waltz.
5. **Potty Training:** The bathroom ballet—essential for a dog's cultured habits.

As we embark on this behavioral symphony, remember: consistent training, positive reinforcement, and socialization compose the notes.

Impact of Repetition: Doggy Deja Vu

Repetition, the DJ of the canine disco, plays a crucial role in making habits stick. Dogs and humans, kindred spirits in learning, groove to the rhythm of reinforcement and consistency. Like a pup DJ dropping the beat, repetition strengthens the neural pathways, turning good behavior into a paws-itively reliable routine. It's the canine equivalent of muscle memory, a groove etched in the dance floor of obedient behavior.

Breaking Bad Habits: A Doggy Intervention

Embarking on the journey of breaking bad habits? Fear not, for recognizing these quirks is the first step. Excessive barking, furniture feasts, and leash acrobatics—common pitfalls, not the mark of a rebellious rover, but a call for better training and communication.

Understanding Triggers: Sherlock Holmes in a Fur Coat

Detective time! Identifying triggers or cues leading to bad habits is elementary, my dear dog owner. Dogs unleash their inner Sherlock, responding to specific situations or stimuli. Spotting these triggers allows you to play the role of proactive detective, addressing issues before they become canine mysteries.

Positive Reinforcement: Treats, Tricks, and Tail Wags

Breaking bad habits becomes a jubilant journey with positive reinforcement. Excessive barker in the house? Reward silence with treats. Over time, your dog connects quietude with goodies, transforming the silence of the woofs.

Gradual Change: Not a Revolution, but an Evolution

Revolution? Too extreme. Think evolution. When facing chronic leash pulling, don't pull a sudden 180. Start with rewards for a polite walk. Increase the time between rewards—voilà, a doggy diplomat emerges.

Case Studies: Tales of Triumph and Transformation

Enter Billy, the jumper. His owner, the maestro of positive reinforcement, turned jumping into sitting for treats and affection. Bravo! Then there's Blair, the anxiety-driven chewer. A symphony of puzzle toys and rewards turned anxiety into calm, and destruction into serenity. Encore!

Reward Systems: A Treat for You, A Treat for Me

Enter the magical realm of rewards—a dual delight for both you and your furry apprentice.

Understanding the Power of Rewards: Wagging Tails and Winning Hearts

Rewards, not just a treat but a proclamation of "Well done!" They create a joyful bond with the training process, injecting fun into learning. For you, the trainer, rewards are the golden keys unlocking cooperation and trust. They're not just treats; they're trusty treaties.

Types of Rewards: A Buffet for the Canine Soul

A reward buffet awaits, catering to the diverse palate of doggy desires.

- **Treats:** The gastronomic delights, but beware the overindulgence buffet.
- **Praise:** Verbal arias and petting symphonies—non-food rewards that resonate.
- **Toys:** A playtime ballet with balls and Frisbee stealing the limelight.
- **Playtime:** The grand finale—spending quality time in the canine carnival.

Choosing the Right Reward: A Symphony of Preferences

Each dog has its taste in rewards. Consider your canine companion's preferences—a symphony personalized for their delight.

Balancing Rewards: Dodging the Indulgence Avalanche

Balance, the tightrope walker of the reward system. Too much, and obesity knocks; too little, and the doggy DJ refuses to spin without treats. Strike the balance, and the dance of obedience begins.

Celebrating Milestones: A Paw-some Party

Setting milestones isn't just for humans. Dogs revel in the journey. Keep the training journey on track with milestones as guideposts.

Tracking Progress: The Canine Chronicle

Dive into the doggy diary! Keep a journal, roll those video cameras, or employ apps and tools. Monitor progress like a hawk—patterns unfold, improvement areas illuminate.

Importance of Celebration: Cheers to Small Wins!

Celebrations aren't reserved for grand victories. Small wins build confidence, deepen bonds, and make training a joyous carnival.

Creating a Reward Calendar: A Symphony of Consistency

Enter the organized realm of calendars. Set a schedule, list rewards, and assign them judiciously. The reward calendar ensures your dog dances to a consistent beat of positive reinforcement.

Incorporating Personal Rewards: Trainer, Treat Thyself

Trainers deserve treats too! Set personal goals—consistency, communication finesse, or mastering new tricks. When achieved, savor a personal treat. A happy trainer is a motivated maestro.

Positive Feedback Loop: Wagging Tails, Learning Trails

In the orchestra of dog training, feedback takes center stage. Rewards create a loop of positivity, reinforcing good behavior. A well-timed treat or pat is the standing ovation, making the encore inevitable.

Creating a Bond: The Heartbeat of Harmony

Rewards aren't just treats; they're the heartbeat of the bond between you and your dog.

Motivation and Progress: Tails Up, Heads High

Motivation, the maestro's baton, keeps the doggy symphony alive. Rewards tap into intrinsic motivation, fueling enthusiasm and steady progress. Training becomes a rhythmic dance of success.

Sustaining Enthusiasm: The Canine Carnival Continues

To keep the training carnival vibrant:

1. **Variety:** Change the tune, switch locations, add new commands—a doggy dance of variety.
2. **Short and Frequent Sessions:** Like a doggy DJ's remix—short, frequent sessions beat long, exhausting ones.
3. **Playtime:** A play break amid training keeps the carnival energy high.
4. **Challenge:** Gradually up the ante, challenging your dog's mental and physical faculties. Boredom? Banished!

There you have it—a symphony of wisdom, humor, and a dash of canine charisma. Let the training carnival continue its paws-itively delightful performance!

Maintaining Momentum

The Importance of Variety

In the grand theater of dog training, monotony is the arch-enemy, and variety is the superhero caping up for the rescue mission. Why, you ask? Behold, the comedy of training plateaus awaits our four-legged apprentices!

1. **Preventing Plateaus:** Just like us humans, dogs hit a plateau if the training routine is as predictable as yesterday's kibble. Cue the yawns and eye rolls. Variety is the script doctor, keeping the learning plot line intriguing and ever-evolving.
2. **Mental Stimulation:** Variety isn't just the spice of life; it's the gourmet feast for your dog's brain. Picture it as a mental gymnastics routine, with new challenges and tasks doing cartwheels to keep their neurons nimble and giggling.
3. **Generalization:** Imagine your dog as a thespian learning to perform in different settings. Variety in training environments teaches them that "sit" isn't just for the living room; it's a Broadway hit adaptable to parks, beaches, and even indoor theaters.
4. **Enhancing Focus:** New exercises are the stand-up comedians of the training world, capturing your dog's attention like the headliner stealing the show. Enhanced focus means better performances, and let's face it, a doggy stand-up routine is always a hit.

Preventing Boredom: The Comedy Roast of Monotony

Monotony and dog training—a pairing more disastrous than a cat and a bubble bath. Here's the lowdown on why keeping it lively is canine comedy gold:

1. **Decreased Motivation:** Picture this: your dog, once the eager understudy, now channeling their inner diva with a disinterested stare. Boredom sabotages motivation, turning training sessions into a canine soap opera—cue the dramatic sighs.
2. **Loss of Enthusiasm:** A bored dog is the equivalent of a Shakespearean tragedy—less likely to deliver a soliloquy of enthusiasm in training. Enthusiasm is the secret sauce; without it, the training plot line loses its sparkle.
3. **Frustration:** Monotony-induced frustration, the sitcom nobody signed up for. Both you and your dog grappling with lackluster progress and engagement—it's the training version of a cliffhanger you'd rather skip.

Incorporating New Challenges: The Comedy Improv Session

Welcome to the improv night of dog training, where new challenges and tasks take center stage, and spontaneity reigns supreme:

1. **Progressive Difficulty:** Like a skilled comedian testing new material, gradually up the difficulty of exercises. Basic commands? Been there, aced that. Now, let's talk about the agility course—a comedy of jumps, twists, and turns.
2. **Advanced Commands:** Move over, basic commands. It's time for the advanced command stand-up hour. Teach your dog tricks that would make Houdini jealous or tasks so specialized, they'd earn a standing ovation at any canine award show.
3. **Problem-Solving Tasks:** Enter the Sherlock Holmes of training—problem-solving exercises. Puzzle toys, scent work—turn your dog into the canine detective, solving mysteries and earning treats as the grand finale.
4. **Change of Environment:** Think of it as a training world tour.

From your backyard to the local park, each location is a different chapter in your dog's training saga. Variety, after all, is the spice of the canine theatrical life.

Rotating Activities: The Training Carnival of Laughter

Enter the training carnival, where laughter is the currency, and variety is the headliner:

1. **Weekly Themes:** Monday is agility day, Wednesday is obedience night, and Friday is all about scent work. Implementing weekly themes keeps the training carnival buzzing with anticipation.
2. **Change Training Locations:** It's the ultimate training travelogue. Backyard one day, local park the next—because why limit your dog to one stage when the whole world is their training arena?
3. **Mix and Match:** A canine variety show—start with basic commands, throw in some agility obstacles, and wrap it up with a fetch finale. The audience (your dog) deserves a diverse performance.
4. **Seasonal Training:** Adjust the training script according to the seasons. Summer? Water-related activities. Fall? Scent work amidst the crunchy leaves. It's the seasonal sitcom your dog never knew they needed.

Community Support: The Canine Comedy Club

In the doggy comedy club, community support is the standing ovation—loud, thunderous, and filled with shared laughter and knowledge:

Joining or creating a community of dog owners and trainers transforms the solo act of training into a comedic ensemble. Benefits? More than a bag of treats!

Communities provide a platform for dog owners and trainers to share their collective knowledge. It's the ultimate open mic night where experiences, techniques, and insights are the punchlines to success.

When the training plot takes a comedic twist, the community is the laugh track. Encouragement, advice, and empathetic responses—it's the supportive audience every trainer deserves.

Seeing other members' progress? It's the motivation comedy special, inspiring you to perfect your own routine and aim for a standing ovation.

Sharing Experiences: The Hilarity of Doggy Anecdotes

Encouraging the sharing of experiences isn't just storytelling; it's a comedy roast where successes and challenges take center stage:

By sharing your own doggy tales, you're not just entertaining the audience; you're providing valuable insights that others can learn from. It's the comedy of shared experiences.

Training challenges become a collective improv session. New perspectives, strategies, and maybe a few doggy jokes thrown in—it's the recipe for overcoming hurdles.

Sharing experiences creates a canine camaraderie. You're not alone in this training sitcom; others are navigating the same comedic twists and turns.

Accountability Partners: Comedy Duets for Consistency

In the comedy duet of training, accountability partners are the perfect scene partners:

They keep you on track, set training goals, and make sure you don't skip rehearsals. The comedy of accountability prevents procrastination, ensuring you deliver the punchlines consistently.

Knowing someone is counting on you to train regularly? It's the comedic pressure you need to shine. Feedback, constructive criticism—comedy is a collaborative art, after all.

Workshops and Classes: The Comedy School of Training

Workshops and classes aren't just training sessions; they're the stand-up specials led by experienced trainers:

Structured programs, like a well-written comedy script, offer a systematic approach to skill development. Dogs become the stars, and trainers? They're the seasoned directors of the comedy show.

Dogs, the social butterflies of the comedy world, get to mingle with other canine comedians and their humans. It's a supervised party where social skills take center stage.

Picture it as improv classes for dogs and their owners. Laughter, learning, and shared experiences—workshops and classes are the comedy clubs where everyone's a member.

Led by professional trainers, these sessions aren't just comedy open mics; they're the headlining acts. Hands-on guidance, expert advice, and a few training jokes—comedy with a purpose.

Staying Consistent: The Comedy Routine of Predictability

Consistency, the comedy routine that never gets old. It's not a one-time gig; it's the sitcom with reruns that dogs adore:

Dogs thrive on predictability, and consistency is their favorite recurring episode. Once you've taught them the script, stick to it like a loyal sidekick.

Inconsistent training? It's the plot twist nobody asked for. Dogs get confused, and confusion in a sitcom is like a laugh track gone wrong.

Even after the standing ovation, it's not curtains down. The encore of refresher sessions is where consistency takes a bow:

Periodic refresher training keeps your dog sharp, like a seasoned comedian fine-tuning their set. Reviewing known commands is the greatest hits album they never get tired of.

Reviewing and reinforcing? It's the comedy of reminding your dog that their training isn't a one-hit wonder. Regular practice maintains those neural pathways, preventing forgetfulness.

Just like humans and punchlines, dogs can forget. Keep those commands fresh, and you'll never have a forgettable performance.

Preventing regression is like ensuring your sitcom stays on the air. Consistency is the script, and positive reinforcement is the laugh track:

Short, focused training sessions are the sitcom episodes. Consistent expectations are the punchlines. It's the comedy duo that prevents regression and keeps the show running smoothly.

Positive reinforcement, the standing ovation your dog craves. Treats, praise, and play—the comedic trio that motivates your dog and keeps their training enthusiasm at its peak.

Commitment is the comedy marathon you signed up for, and it's worth every laugh:

Set a regular training schedule, even if it's as short as a sitcom episode. Consistency in timing keeps you and your dog on the same comedic wavelength.

Busy life? It's the comedy ensemble—involve family members, hire a dog trainer, or bring in the comedic relief of training aids and tools. Because in this comedy, the show must go on.

The Power of Goal Setting

Setting new goals is the comedy plot twist that keeps the training sitcom fresh and exciting:

Goals are the script, offering a direction for your training journey. Achieving each goal? It's the punchline that brings joy and motivates you to pen the next scene.

Dogs age, and so does the comedy script. Adapt your goals to suit their stage of life. It's the improv session where the script evolves with the actor.

Life changes? It's the comedy writers' room—adjust goals to accommodate new plot lines. Flexibility keeps the training sitcom from becoming a predictable rerun.

What's the series finale of your training sitcom? Define your long-term vision:

Break it down into achievable goals—the episodic journey to the grand finale. Celebrate each milestone, because in this comedy, the journey is the destination.

Highlighting achievements is the comedy curtain call, celebrating the hilarious journey of training:

Celebrate past successes, sure. But don't forget to pop the champagne for new milestones. Each achievement is a comedic scene-stealer, and the audience (you and your dog) deserves a standing ovation.

A lifetime of dog training isn't just a sitcom; it's a canine comedy masterpiece. Laughter, shared adventures, enduring friendship—it's the script of joy, commitment, and the extraordinary bond forged through training. In this narrative, every training session is a comedic act, a testament to patience, compassion, and the remarkable power of a dog's heart. Cheers to the comedy of training, where every cue, command, and canine caper is a punchline that echoes in the halls of laughter and love.*

You're all set to create an enriching life for your dog and yourself.

11

Conclusion

Effective dog training methods are based on positive reinforcement, clear communication, and consistency. A key component of successful training is the "10-minute rule," which emphasizes short, focused training sessions. This approach optimizes learning, prevents boredom, and maintains a dog's motivation.

Positive reinforcement is at the core of effective dog training. It involves rewarding your dog for desired behaviors, reinforcing the connection between the action and the reward. This method promotes a positive, encouraging atmosphere and builds trust between the dog and the trainer.

Clear communication is equally important. Using consistent cues and commands helps your dog understand what you expect. Simple, unambiguous instructions are easier for your dog to grasp and execute. Consistency ensures that your dog recognizes the signals and can respond correctly.

Consistency extends beyond cues; it also pertains to the training environment and the timing of rewards. A regular training schedule and a consistent set of rules at home help your dog generalize the training to different situations.

The "10-minute rule" is a valuable strategy in effective dog training. Training sessions should be kept short and focused, lasting around 10 minutes. These concentrated sessions help maintain your dog's attention and prevent mental fatigue. Frequent short sessions are more productive than infrequent, lengthy ones. These bite-sized training moments keep your dog engaged and eager to learn.

The "10-minute rule" aligns with a dog's natural attention span. Dogs can concentrate on a specific task for about 10-15 minutes, making shorter, frequent training sessions highly effective. Beyond the training session, you can reinforce the lessons throughout the day by practicing behaviors in different contexts.

In conclusion, effective dog training methods center around positive reinforcement, clear communication, and consistency. The "10-minute rule" complements these techniques, ensuring that training sessions are engaging, productive, and conducive to your dog's natural learning abilities. By following these principles, you can build a strong foundation for a well-behaved and happy canine companion.

Continue applying these methods

Now that you've learned about effective dog training methods, it's time to put your knowledge into action. The well-being and behavior of your furry companion depend on consistent, positive, and clear training. Start by incorporating short, focused training sessions using the "10-minute rule." Remember the power of positive reinforcement and maintain clear communication with your dog. Create a training schedule that fits your lifestyle, ensuring consistency in your approach. By applying these methods consistently, you'll not only have a well-behaved and happy dog, but you'll also strengthen the bond between you and your loyal companion. Take action now and enjoy the rewards of a harmonious partnership with your four-legged friend.

What's Next: Resources for further study.

Here are some valuable resources for further study on effective dog training methods:

1. Books:

- "The Power of Positive Dog Training" by Pat Miller: A comprehensive guide to positive reinforcement training.

- "Don't Shoot the Dog: The New Art of Teaching and Training" by Karen Pryor: Explores the principles of operant conditioning and positive reinforcement.

2. Online Courses:

- Coursera offers courses on dog training and behavior.

- Udemy has a range of courses on dog training, from basic obedience to advanced techniques.

3. Websites:

- American Kennel Club (AKC): The AKC provides valuable resources on dog training and offers a list of certified trainers.

- Association of Professional Dog Trainers (APDT): APDT offers information on positive dog training techniques and a directory of certified trainers.

4. YouTube Channels:

- Zak George's Dog Training Revolution: Zak George shares numerous training videos and tips.

- Kikopup: Emily Larlham offers a wide range of positive reinforcement training videos.

5. Podcasts:

- Canine Nation: A podcast that explores dog training, behavior, and science-based techniques.

- The Dog Trainer's Quick and Dirty Tips for Teaching and Caring for Your Pet: Offers quick and practical dog training and care tips.

6. Local Dog Training Classes: Check with local dog training facilities or trainers who offer classes, workshops, and one-on-one sessions.

7. Dog Training Forums and Communities: Online forums like Reddit's r/Dog training or various Facebook groups dedicated to dog training are great places to seek advice and share experiences with fellow dog owners and trainers.

Remember, effective dog training is an ongoing journey that requires continuous learning and adaptation. Explore these resources, attend classes, and engage with the dog training community to enhance your skills and ensure a harmonious relationship with your canine companion.

* * *

Continuing the Training Journey

Now that you've completed your journey through "10-Minute Dog Training Essentials" and acquired valuable insights into science-backed training methods that work, it's time to pay it forward and help other fellow dog enthusiasts on their training adventures. By sharing your honest thoughts and experiences with this book on Amazon, you can guide other dog owners towards a resource that can transform their relationship with their furry companions and make their training journey smoother.

Your review is a beacon for those seeking knowledge and guidance in the world of dog training. Your words can inspire and empower others to embark on this rewarding path and strengthen the bond they share with their four-legged friends. Remember, the canine community thrives when we pass on our wisdom and passion; your review is vital to that process.

Thank you for your support and dedication to the world of dog training. Your contribution ensures that dog training continues to grow and evolve, improving the lives of countless dogs and their owners. To share your review and extend a helping paw to fellow dog lovers, click the link below or scan the QR code:

Scan or click here to leave a review

Your generosity in sharing your thoughts is deeply appreciated. To-gether, we're making a positive impact on the world of dog training, one review at a time.

About the Author

Andi Dencklau has spent a lifetime in the company of dogs, forging an unbreakable bond with these loyal companions. With over four decades of experience as a devoted dog enthusiast, Andi brings a wealth of knowledge and a passion for canine well-being to the world of dog training.

As a certified animal aromacologist, certified trick dog trainer, and a former veterinarian technician, Andi's expertise extends beyond training into the realm of holistic pet care. This unique blend of skills has allowed Andi to understand dogs on a profound level, from their physical health to their emotional needs.

Andi's love for dogs has manifested in various forms, from competing in agility, dock diving, herding, and trick dog training to serving as an agility judge. This hands-on experience has provided invaluable insights into the world of dog training and behavior.

Driven by a deep desire to share this wealth of knowledge, Andi Dencklau authored "10-Minute Dog Training Essentials." This book is a culmination of years of experience, a dedication to positive training methods, and a genuine commitment to helping dog owners and their beloved pets lead happier, healthier lives together.

Andi Dencklau's mission is to empower dog owners with the tools they need to build strong, loving relationships with their furry companions through effective and compassionate training techniques. With "10-Minute Dog Training Essentials," Andi invites you on a journey to unlock the potential of your canine partner and discover the joy of harmonious companionship.

You can connect with me on:
- https://bordercolliepassion.com
- https://www.facebook.com/bordercolliepassion

Subscribe to my newsletter:
- https://bordercolliepassion.com

Also by Andi Dencklau

In addition to "10-Minute Dog Training Essentials," Andi Dencklau has a remarkable body of work that reflects a deep commitment to animals and their well-being. With a career dedicated to understanding and advocating for our four-legged friends, Andi has authored several books that offer invaluable insights into the world of animal care and training. Here are a few:

Beyond the Rainbow Bridge: Actionable Steps to Healing Your Grieving Heart

Losing a cherished pet leaves an indelible mark on your heart, and the path to healing can seem daunting. In "Beyond the Rainbow Bridge," Andi, a devoted pet owner for over 45 years, offers a compassionate guide to navigating the complexities of pet loss grief.

This book is a heartfelt companion for those who are seeking solace in their pain, providing practical and actionable steps to help you heal your grieving heart. Andi understands the unique pain points of losing a beloved pet, and she shares insights and strategies to address your grief directly.

"Beyond the Rainbow Bridge" helps you comprehend why your grief for your pet is unique and why your feelings are valid, examines the emotional, physical, and psychological reactions that often accompany pet loss and offers validation for your experiences.

It provides actionable steps for emotional healing, including exercises, reflections, and strategies to navigate your grief while exploring ways to honor and remember your pet, offering creative ideas for memorials and keepsakes.

"Beyond the Rainbow Bridge" guides you in finding a new normal, addressing potential feelings of guilt, and understanding the role of a new pet in your life when the time is right.

Andi's profound insights, drawn from her own experiences, create a bridge of empathy between author and reader. Her words serve as a source of solace, understanding, and hope for those who seek to heal their grieving hearts. "Beyond the Rainbow Bridge" is a practical and empathetic guide for anyone facing the profound loss of a beloved pet.

Andi Dencklaw

Beginner's Guide to Raising and Loving a Well-Behaved Border Collie

Are you thinking about welcoming a Border Collie into your life but don't know where to start? Perhaps you've heard that these intelligent dogs can be a handful if not trained properly? Look no further!

"Beginner's Guide to Raising and Loving a Well-Behaved Border Collie" is your ultimate guide to understanding, training, and nurturing this wonderful breed.

What's included in this guide:

Unlock the Secret to a Well-Behaved Border Collie: From basic obedience commands to advanced training techniques, we've got you covered.

Master Early Socialization: Understand the importance and methods of early socialization to shape a well-rounded dog.

Decode Your Dog's Nutrition: Whether it's commercial dog food or a raw diet, get the scoop on what's best for your Border Collie.

Be Prepared for Health Issues: Learn about common Border Collie-specific health concerns and how to address them.

Holistic Care Options: Dive into alternative therapies like aromatherapy and acupuncture to enhance your dog's well-being.

This book is designed for both first-time dog owners and seasoned Border Collie enthusiasts. While border collies are energetic and intelligent, our detailed guidance will help you channel their energy productively.

Don't miss out on making the most rewarding journey with your Border

Collie. Click the "Buy Now" button to embark on this incredible adventure of raising a well-behaved, happy, and healthy dog!

Unlock the full potential of your relationship with your Border Collie—invest in this indispensable guide today!

Canine First Aid Made Easy: Saving Dogs, Saving Money, and Easing Your Stress - Your Essential Pet First Aid Guide

Every dog owner knows their furry friend isn't just a pet; they're a beloved family member. In "Canine First Aid Made Easy: Saving Dogs, Saving Money, and Easing Your Stress - Your Essential Pet First Aid Guide," you'll find essential knowledge and skills needed to be your dog's first responder in times of crisis.

Whether you're a seasoned dog owner or a new puppy parent, this comprehensive guide is your indispensable companion for ensuring your canine companion's health and safety. This invaluable resource takes you on a journey through the world of canine first aid, offering expert advice and step-by-step instructions to handle a wide range of emergencies and health concerns.

You'll learn how to assess your dog's vital signs, recognize distress, and take immediate action when it matters most. Discover the secrets to building a well-equipped canine first aid kit, tailored to your dog's unique needs, and learn how to use it effectively in emergency situations. From common injuries like cuts and sprains to critical issues such as choking, poisoning, or even cardiac emergencies, this guide provides clear and concise instructions to help you stay calm and make the right decisions under pressure.

Inside "Canine First Aid," you'll find:
Detailed guidance on assessing your dog's vital signs, including temperature, pulse, and respiration.
Easy-to-follow instructions for handling common emergencies such as choking, poisoning, and heatstroke.

Wound care and bandaging techniques to minimize infection and promote healing.

Insights into gastrointestinal issues, respiratory problems, cardiovascular emergencies, and more.

Tips for identifying and responding to neurological, eye, ear, skin, and dental problems.

Guidance on reproductive and urinary issues, as well as special considerations for working dogs.

Practical advice for disaster preparedness, preventive care, and maintaining your dog's health.

Helpful appendices featuring first aid kit checklists, emergency contact information, and common medications.

Written by experts in veterinary care and first aid, "Canine First Aid" is your go-to resource for becoming a proactive and confident caretaker of your beloved canine companion. With this book in hand, you'll gain the knowledge and skills to provide essential care and potentially save your dog's life in critical moments.

Made in the USA
Monee, IL
13 November 2024

69883277R00134